SILVER BIRCH

A SPECIAL PLACE TO LIVE

BY

DAWN E WEST

*Dedicated to my children Alan,
Jason and Shannon. And my Parents.*

"The essential joy of being with horses is that it brings us in contact with the rare elements of grace, beauty, spirit and fire."

Sharon Ralls Lemon

CHAPTER ONE

It was the beginning of another busy day, at The Silver Birch Riding School. Today, was the local Pony Show, and many of the horses would be attending. Helping was a young girl called Phoebe Adams, whose parents owned the School.

As Phoebe and her friends, were busy gathering the tack they would be needing for the day. Phoebe's Mum, who was called Lauren, was busy helping a pony, who was having problems with being loaded onto one of the trailers.

She was an experienced Horse Trainer, who had been to America, and was taught by a famous Horse Whisperer at his Ranch in Montana. Where she learned all about the handling and training of horses, so was able to give, the encouragement they needed.

It was during her time there, that she met Phoebe's Dad, Reece Adams. He was a Stunt Rider who had been in many Films, and could train any horse that seemed to be highly strung, or just needing gentle handling. Together, they made a great team. Phoebe, who had the same passion for horses as them, wanted to ride in the Olympics one day. But for now, the local Pony Shows would do. As soon as everyone was ready, the horses loaded, they were on their way.

In the horsebox being driven by Mum, was Shetland Ponies Teddy and Lolly, and a Pony called Barney, that all belonged to Phoebe. Dad followed behind with the horses he would be using, in a Spectacular Stunt Show.

The sun was shining brightly as they arrived, even though there was a cold chill in the air.

With the horseboxes parked, they began unloading. Mum came out with Barney, and the two little Shetlands. Lolly a miniature, who was bought as a Show Pony. Looked pretty with her tail and mane plaited with red coloured ribbons, as she stood alongside Teddy. Who never had the greatest start in life.

He had been tied in a field for days, never seeing a friendly face. Until he was eventually saved by a kind lady, who took him back to her home, which was a Rescue Centre for horses and ponies. This is where her parents had seen him, and decided to give, the loving home he deserved.

Lolly, who was very small compared to him, has been the perfect companion.

There were lots of people, that had turned up to compete at the Show. Phoebe herself, had been entered in two of the Events, and her first would be in the Novice Jumping.

Phoebe wasted no time and started to get ready, she would be riding Barney for the Show. He was a Welsh Cob, with a very distinct golden mane and tail, and had been bought by her parents as a birthday present.

As she finished putting on her riding hat, Phoebe walked over to her parents who wished her luck, and went with her to look at the Course.

The jumps were much smaller than in the Advanced Class, and looked quite easy to follow.

"Just do the best you can honey, and take it easy." said Dad, as he showed her the best way to take the jumps.

Suddenly, they heard a voice saying that the first Class will be starting shortly. So Phoebe mounted Barney, and took him to the exercise area, to get him warmed up, ready to go in the Ring. When she arrived, she met with her friends Casey, Megan, Louise and Rebecca.

Who attended the same School. They all had their ponies in livery at Silver Birch, apart from Rebecca. She lived in a big house in the nearby Village, which had its own stables.

"Hey Phoebe, are you still going to The County Show next Sunday?" asked Casey, as she came alongside on her pony called Ruby.

"Yes l will be, l want to get as much experience as l can before the Shows finish." She replied.

"I hope we do well today, l haven't done much since Hettys leg strain." Louise sighed. As she looked down at her pony, whilst trying to place her reins around her fingers.

The friends all wished each other luck, and waited in the exercise area to be called. As the ponies enjoyed a few minutes warming up. It was soon Phoebe's turn to enter the Ring.

Her adrenalin rushing through her body, she tried her best to keep composed for Barney. And as the bell rang, Phoebe began her first jump...

Barney took it all in his stride, he loved being in the Ring and it showed. He had the experience of all Equestrian Sports, and was turning out to be a good teacher for Phoebe, who needed an experienced pony.

Soon they were over the first few fences. Phoebe knew that if she didn't knock any of the jumps down, they may have a chance to get a clear round. But as she tightened her grip ready for the next jump, Barney clipped the top of the pole!!

Phoebe looked round quickly, but the pole managed to stay in place. Breathing a sigh of relief, she couldn't believe her luck.

Phew !! that was close she thought, as her heart was pounding...

"Concentrate Phoebe.' She told herself.

Gathering herself together, they continued to the next few jumps, until there was just one left to go. Barney jumped magnificently, and cleared this with ease, everyone clapped and cheered. Phoebe was delighted as she gave Barney a big hug.

"Well done." Rebecca said, as she was just about to enter.

"Thanks Becks." Phoebe replied, and trotted Barney out.

Jumping from the saddle, she walked him over to the horsebox, so he could get a well deserved drink, when Mum came running over.

"Phoebe, you were within the time, and you cleared every jump!!" She said.

"There's a good chance you might get first place!!" added Mum, who was so thrilled.

As they waited to see the results, it was clear that Phoebe and Barney had got a first placing.

With all the excitement, of the first event, Mum nearly forgot The Shetland Pony Race that Teddy was entered in.

As they both rushed over to the horsebox, where Teddy had been waiting patiently with Lolly.

Phoebe, quickly grabbed herself a sandwich from the picnic basket, that Mum had put together earlier, and began to saddle him up.

"I'll take you for a quick walk first." Phoebe told him.

Placing a coloured band around her arm, which was bright pink with blue stars, she walked him over to the start, where all the other ponies were waiting.

Teddy loved being at the Shows, especially because of all the attention he received, which was normally from Children. They loved him, because he was just their size, and would give him lots of cuddles and peppermint treats.

As the riders mounted their ponies, the whistle sounded....

Off Phoebe and Teddy went !!

Galloping along, with the wind blowing through his mane and tail, Teddy headed towards the first flagpole, where a ribbon had been tied. Phoebe with all her strength, grabbed at the ribbon, and pulled it from the pole.

"Quick Ted !!" She shrieked.

"let's get to the next one!!"

Phoebe held on tight, she could see the other riders coming up fast. Harry, a boy from School, came by on his Shetland called Bertie. Phoebe knew then, that if she played it right, they could at least make third place.

"Come on Boy!! "Phoebe shouted.

"Let's get to the finishing line!!" With that, Teddy mustered all his energy to keep in third.

Over the finishing line they went, as Phoebe screamed with delight, telling him how great he had done.

Taking Teddy by the reins, she walked him back to the horsebox. Lolly, who had been waiting so patiently for him to return, made a loud neighing noise like if to say, *'Where have you been'.*

"I'm sure she talks to you Ted." Phoebe said, while taking off his saddle, as Lolly nuzzled up to him.

After making sure Teddy was settled, she went to watch the jumping in the Advance Class. Phoebe always dreamt of being in a higher class, but for now all she could do was just watch.

The jumps in the Advance Ring, were much higher than the Novice. And the horses needed to be really fit, to achieve a clear round in the allocated time. With horses being ridden round so quickly, and with such ease, it was exciting and thrilling to watch.

Suddenly Mum came along with Lolly, who had been entered in the *'Best Pony Competition'.* Phoebe not wanting to miss Lolly at her first showing, went with mum to watch.

As they got near, Mum gave Lolly one final check to make sure she looked her best, and entered the Ring...

The Judge, looking over this tiny Shetland, asked Mum if she could take Lolly in a circle, so she could see her when walking and trotting.

Lolly looked so sweet, but she never had any problems looking after herself. Just because she was tiny, she could certainly put the larger horses in their places.

Once the Judge had seen all the others, she walked over to Mum carrying a red rosette, which was presented to them as *Best in Show*. Everyone seemed happy with the Judges choice, and gave a huge cheer. Phoebe looked on with great pride, as Lolly made the most of all the attention.

Time was getting on, and soon the Presentations would be awarded. Phoebe went to get Barney, to receive their first place in *Novice Jumping*.

He was given a red rosette, which was placed at the side of his bridle, while Phoebe, was presented with a book token. Her other friends Casey, Rebecca and Louise, all got placed respectfully.

Phoebe went to collect Teddy for his Class, But he was busy munching on his hay when she arrived.

"Come on Ted, you can leave your food for a second." She told him. Pulling him away from the only thing he was more interested in.

As they finally went to receive their award, for third place in the Racing. Phoebe thought, it had not been a bad day for the ponies, they would all be going home with something. At the horsebox, Mum and Phoebe made sure the ponies were all settled, before going to see her father.

Making their way to the Stands, they could hear the noise from the Crowds, and were amazed to see just how many people, that had come to watch.

As silence fell over the Arena, everyone waited in anticipation for the Show to start...

When the music began to play, out came Phoebe's Dad, on a big grey horse called Apollo.

Riding at such speed, with his feet out of the stirrups, he began to slide off the saddle holding on with just one hand!!

As he moved his body, from one side of the horse to the other, he rode around the Arena, with his head, barely inches from the ground!!

The audience gasped at such a dangerous stunt.

Dad soon came to a halt in the centre, and introduced himself to the Crowds...

"Howdy Folks, hope your all gonna enjoy the show we have for you tonight, thank you for coming." He said, as Apollo reared up on his hind legs...

In the distance, Phoebe could see two men carrying large wooden rings, which they placed in a large circle. As the men set fire to each ring, they quickly moved away.

The rings became engulfed with flames, as the colours of yellows, oranges and reds, lit up the evening sky. Dad, then informed the astonished Crowd, he was going to jump through The Rings *Of Fire!!*

A sound of a drum roll could be heard, as he began to ride Apollo around the outer ring. Around and around they went, until he reached the first Ring of Fire....

Through the flames they jumped!!

Apollo showing he had every confidence and trust in her father. Everyone held their breath, and as Apollo came through the last ring. The place erupted as everyone clapped and cheered !!

"Thank you, Thank you!!" shouted Dad, to the Crowd. And went on to do even more daring stunts for them.

Suddenly, the spotlights shone in the direction of where a huge black Friesian horse called Axel, was standing. And as he made his way into the Arena, there was a loud cheer.

He had worked with her father on many films, and had become a star in his own right. For a horse, he was pretty amazing. As he galloped over towards where Dad was standing, his black coat glistened as the lights shone upon him, he looked every inch the star!!

When he reached her father he was told to lie down, and as he did so, Dad climbed upon his saddle. Axel began to do many tricks which included, dancing to music, and even riding through a wall of fire!!

Soon it was time for the big finale, which was too involve both horses being ridden at the same time!!

Everyone stood up clapping and cheering, as these two magnificent horses galloped around, while Dad stood on their backs holding just one set of reins!!

The Show had been spectacular, and for the Audience, so exciting to see, it had been a great success.

Phoebe and Mum went back stage to see Dad, as crowds gathered, just to get a glimpse of all the horses that had taken part in the Show.

Taking the horses back to the horsebox, they were given some water. Dad started to unsaddle them, ready for the long drive home.

People still tried to get a look at these wonderful horses, and to ask about the films that Dad had been associated with. Phoebe watched, as he made the effort to try and talk to everyone, and allowed them to take pictures, of Axel and Apollo. Time went by quickly, so Dad decided to start loading the horses.

Teddy and Lolly, looked like they had already fallen asleep. It was funny the way they seem to be leaning on each other. Yawning herself, Phoebe sat back in the passenger seat looking at all the ribbons, thinking to herself... One day people will know me as, *Phoebe Adams Olympic Champion.* And with that, she gradually fell asleep.

When they finally reached home, Mum gently woke her by nudging her arm. Phoebe gave a big yawn, stretching her arms up in the air, she gradually helped with unloading the ponies. Making a big fuss of them all, she put Barney out in the paddocks, and sat watching her Mum, take the plaits out of Lollys mane and tail.

"We were so proud of you today, especially when you went into the Novice Ring." Mum told her.

Phoebe looked at her, and smiled.

"It was all down to the ponies, they did well." She said. Looking at Teddy, as she walked him into the stable. She knew, that was where he wanted to be, especially when it was cold outside. She didn't blame him, it had turned quite chilly, and he was getting on a bit now.

"Right." said Mum, as she turned to Phoebe while walking Lolly into the stable next to him.

"I am just going to help with the other horses, and I will be straight back to make some tea." And with that, off she went. While Phoebe made her way back to the house.

Once in the kitchen she went over to the Aga, which was like a big oven, that made the kitchen lovely and warm.

Sitting on one of the comfy chairs, Phoebe sat eating a large slice of chocolate cake, when after a while her parents came in...

"Let's have a piece of that cake, it looks yummy." said Dad, as he grabbed a chair and sat down by the table.

"Of course you can." said Phoebe, jumping up and cutting off a huge slice. Mum made them all hot chocolate to drink. This was Phoebe's favourite, with fresh cream and loads of tiny marshmallows on top. It was lovely and hot, and always made you feel good.

"I will hang the rosettes up in the tack room in a minute." she told Mum.

"But can l give Louise a ring first, just to find out how Hetty is, if that's okay?" She asked.

"Of course." answered Mum.

So, off Phoebe went to phone...

"Hi Mrs Webb, is Louise there?" She asked.

"Is that Phoebe, hold on a minute, l will get her for you." replied Mrs Webb.

Who then called out to Louise, who was busy upstairs, sorting things out for School on Monday. As she came to the phone Phoebe asked how Hetty was.

"She is fine thanks, l am really pleased she did so well." answered Louise. Who was still quite shocked, that Hetty, had managed to get round without any problems.

"I was so surprised that we got fourth place."

Sounding delighted, at the fact she was placed at all.

"I know that Harry got first place in the racing, because he past me." Phoebe replied, adding.

"Still l will let you get on, and I'll catch up with you at School." And with that, put the phone down, and went back into the kitchen.

As she took the last sip of hot chocolate, she grabbed the rosettes taking them outside, to put with all the others, that she had accumulated. Coming out from the stables, she could hear Mum in the distance calling her for dinner. So made a quick dash back to the house.

"Was your hands first." Mum said, as she entered. Phoebe went to get cleaned up, and was soon making her way back to the kitchen.

"Mm... lovely casserole with dumplings." Phoebe said, as she sat down at the table, and tucked in. It was just what was needed on a cold day.

When dinner was over, Phoebe made her way back upstairs to do her homework, ready for School on Monday. There had been an Autumn break, and they had been told to write down their times tables, ready for when they returned.

Math's was not her favourite subject, but she did love History and Drama. At School, they had been on a trip to a Museum, to see Artifacts from Egypt.

She liked her School, it was small and only held around eighty pupils. Some had lived in the village for most of their lives, and some like Phoebe, had come from other Towns.

Phoebe herself, had been born in a village called Epping Green, until her parents bought Silver Birch. Which use to be an old farmhouse, until it was converted into the Equestrian Centre it was today. Surrounded by the open countryside, and nestled inbetween the very trees, that they had taken its name from.

Silver Birch, had become the focus of the village. With Charity Events, and holding its own small Show every Summer, it was known for being a friendly place. Mum would always make the time to help, or give advice to people. And they appreciated that. When Phoebe finished her homework, she placed it in her book bag.

Switching on the Telly, she wanted to catch up with The X Factor, just to see who had gone through to the next round. Wondering, if it had been the young boy called Sam, who had all the girls at School talking about him.

Suddenly, she heard Dad calling from downstairs, saying that he needed help with the horses. Phoebe called out, that she would be down in a minute, and off she went.

Outside was cold, and she could see Axel and Apollo standing by the barn. They looked so huge, being as both of them were just over sixteen hands high.

There was never a dull moment being around such talented animals. Especially, when they were in training for new routines or stunts.

It was exciting to have a Dad, who was always filming somewhere, and had travelled the World. Phoebe herself, had become great friends to some of the children, whose parents were in films. For someone of just ten, she was always very caring and thoughtful, and they appreciated that of her.

Once the horses and the equipment was put away, and the horsebox all cleaned, they headed back to the house. Mum was busy in the kitchen, sorting out the Staff Rota's for the coming week as usual. And asked, if they had already done the horses, as she would have helped, but had so much to do.

"That's okay Mum we were fine, everything is done now." Phoebe told her, as she took off her coat and boots.

"Great, l can finish off here, and then put my feet up." replied Mum, as she continued with her work.
But just as she was about to inform Dad, on some of the things that needed doing around the School.

The phone began to ring.

It was Penny, who owned the Horse Rescue that had helped Teddy. She had become good friends with both of Phoebe's parents.

Penny began to inform her, of a man who was having problems with a young horse he had sold.

Apparently, the horse was not very happy, with the idea of going in the back of a horsebox.

"Could you pop over and see him in the morning, I would be grateful?" She asked.

"That's fine, but it will have to be after one o'clock, as the Farrier is coming." Mum said, looking at her calendar.

"That will be great, he has a place in Throckenholt called 'The Chestnuts.' It's just down a small lane on the right, as you come over the bridge." informed Penny.

"I think I know where that is." Mum replied.

Writing the address down.

"I will see him tomorrow, sometime in the afternoon."

"That will be fine, I'll let him know." replied Penny. Making her way back to the kitchen, Mum informed them it was Penny, and that she needed help with a horse that had a few problems.

"I will have a look tomorrow, and see what I can do."

She said, as she carried on writing her schedules out for the morning. Mum was always so organized, she had to be.

Running Silver Birch was a full time job. With horses in livery, teaching in the Riding School, to fixing fencing. She took it all in her stride. Phoebe knew, it wasn't easy with her Dad being away so much. But Mum had the support from a great bunch of people, that helped her when she needed it.

"Do you want me to deal with Tom, when he comes to do the horses?" asked Dad, as he poured the last of the coffee into his cup.

"No that's ok, I will need to sort out something's with him anyway." Mum replied, as she gathered up her papers.

"Well young lady, time for bed I think." Mum told a yawning Phoebe. Who had been falling asleep on the chair, and was obviously tired.

"It's been a long day." Dad said. "You will need to be up early in the morning."

"Okay, but can l go with you tomorrow when you look at the horse?" asked Phoebe, while sipping on her hot chocolate. Mum looked at her and said she could, but she would need to do her chores first.

At the weekends, Phoebe always helped Mum. She loved helping out, as it gave her a sense of responsibility, and taught her to have respect for the animals that were in their care. Besides, she loved being around the horses, they were always fun to watch. They each had their own characters, especially Teddy and Lolly, they always had Phoebe in fits of laughter.

After helping Mum with the washing up, Phoebe rushed upstairs to bed, to be up bright and early for the next day. As she lay there, she began to think of the Show, and how wonderful it was to see Teddy win a Race. He was getting old now, and was enjoying his life at Silver Birch.

Lately, he was used for the younger children to ride at the School, as he gave them the confidence they needed, just like he had given Phoebe. He meant so much to her, that they would always share a special bond.

Phoebe's thoughts were suddenly interrupted, by the sound of her parents coming upstairs.

"Hey honey, lights out, you have to get up early remember." said Dad, as he peered around the door.

Phoebe said her goodnights, and it wasn't long before she was fast asleep, and dreaming of the excitement of the day.

And what a day it had been, with rosettes all round for the ponies, and her father, who had wowed the crowds with his Stunt Show. She was so proud of him, working with horses always had its dangers. But Dad could handle himself.

CHAPTER TWO

He was born on a Cattle Ranch in Montana, called *The Triple A.* So coming from a family that lived, and breathed horses, he had taught her to ride, when she was only a baby. placing her on one of the ponies, as he walked alongside. Until the day came, when she was confident enough to ride on her own. That's the way he had been taught.

The next morning, Phoebe was woken by the sound of rain hitting against the windows. On opening the curtains she looked outside, and saw that there were puddles everywhere... Teddy wont like this, he hates the rain, he will certainly want to stay in. She thought. As soon as Phoebe was dressed, she went downstairs.

On entering the kitchen, she saw that Alex and Holly were there. They were Riding Instructors, who worked with her mother.

"Hi Phoebe, we heard you did really well at the Show yesterday." Alex said, pouring out a cup of tea.

"Yes, l got placed with Barney in Novice, and received third place with Teddy as well !!"

Phoebe answered all excited.

As Mum gave her breakfast, she reminded her to come outside once she had finished. So they could make a start on cleaning out the animals.

Once she had cleared the last piece of bacon from her plate. Phoebe was putting on her boots and thick coat, and going outside to help Mum.

Teddy and Lolly was already waiting for her by their stables.

"Hi Ted, what's wrong boy?" Phoebe asked, as if she didn't know. He must have spent every waking day out in the rain and snow, before being rescued.

As she cuddled up to him, Teddy kept lifting his head and nudging her. He was not happy that it was wet and damp outside.

"You just don't like the rain do you boy?" Phoebe said. "That's alright Ted, l will find out if you can wait in the barn for the Farrier."

Looking at Barney and Lolly, who were only to impatient to get out in the paddocks. She made her way over to the other side of the yard, where there was a big American barn.

It was built by her father for the horses that he used for stunts, and was an exact replica, of the one back home in Montana.

As she went inside, Phoebe called out to him.

He was busy cleaning out the stalls as usual with Josh. Who was an American, and came from Montana just like her father. And was a Stunt Rider too.

He had been in many films, and was a real Cowboy, who still wore his trademark hat and boots.

"Howdy Phoebe." Josh said, tilting his hat slightly. Nodding her head, she turned to Dad, asking if she could keep Teddy in the barn, until at least the rain had stopped.

Dad turned to her and said that was fine. He knew what Teddy had been through, everyone did. Phoebe made her way back to where Teddy was waiting, with Lolly and Barney.

It was nearly one o'clock, and the Riding School was busy with children and adults learning to ride as usual.

"The Farrier will be here soon, so let's get the horses out into the yard." Mum said rushing to get ready.

Phoebe was brushing Teddy when he arrived, driving a big blue van, that carried all the tools that he would need.

"Hello Tom." said Mum walking over to him, as he was putting on his leather apron.

"Do you wish to see Teddy and Lolly first?" She asked. Tom grabbing his trimming tools, said that he would prefer to do the Shetlands first, as they will only need a quick trim.

While Phoebe stood with Teddy, as Tom trimmed his hooves. Teddy, found this very ticklish indeed, his bottom lip quivered as if he was laughing.

Ted was very good with Tom, he had known him for quite a few years now, and held his feet up with no problems.

Tom was a good friend to her parents, as he was always giving them advice, especially where it concerned horses. It was because of his knowledge, that he began working on numerous film sets, as Farrier for the Stunt horses. And would normally travel to wherever her father was filming.

Lolly was next, her hooves were the tiniest, and like most girls loved the attention that was made of her. When he finished, Tom gave them both a sugar cube as always for good behaviour. Barney didn't need anything done, his shoes were fine, so Tom went to look at the larger horses, in case they needed shoeing.

As he continued to work, Phoebe gave Teddy some hay and placed it inside the barn door. Then grabbing Lolly, placed her bright pink rug on, and took her over to join Barney, and the other horses in the paddocks.

Mum called over to Phoebe again, and told her to hurry up if she wanted to go with her. Phoebe asked, if she could just run in and collect a few things, as she wanted to go to her friend's house on the way back.

"Quickly then." said Mum looking at her watch.

Time was getting on, and she always liked to be punctual. Knowing it would be a long drive to Throckenholt, Mum decided to play the Abba CD, that Dad had bought for her Birthday. Scince seeing 'Mama Mia' at the Cinema, Mum was always going around singing the songs.

As they continued down the country lanes, all you could hear was the sounds of *'Dancing Queen'* coming from the car. Until, finally reaching the house they were looking for.

"Here it is Mum." Phoebe said, pointing at a lovely thatched cottage. "The Chestnuts."

At the side, was a driveway that took you to where the stable yard was. Mum headed towards where the man was waiting, and introduced herself...

"Hi my name is Lauren, l was told by Penny you needed help with a horse?"

"Yes that's right, his over here." The man turned and said. And with that, they followed him to where a horse was tied to a post. He was a beautiful Piebald Cob, with a long wavy mane and tail. And being about three years, had a terrible fear of being loaded onto something, he had not been on before.

"I try and load him, but he bucks and kicks out." said the man as he untied him.

Mum asked that they all move back, as it was much easier to work one to one. But she was also aware, that it could be very dangerous. Working with horses was always unpredictable, even she had been on the receiving end of a disgruntled horse. After sometime, the horse seemed totally different. Looking calm, as Mum walked him onto the trailer.

"There you go he is fine now, you shouldn't have anymore trouble loading him." She told the man. "But l will leave you my number just in case." Mum added.

The man was very pleased, and said his thanks while walking them back to their car.

As they drove back through the tiny country lanes, they neared the village of Leverington. Where Phoebe was left, at her friend's house.

"I will pick you up around six." Mum told her.

"Okay." She called back waving goodbye.

With a knock on the door, Phoebe waited for someone to answer...

"Hi there Phoebe." Rebecca said. Opening the door, as she tried desperately to get the rubber bands out from her hair.

"I have just come back from riding Blaze." She added. Rebecca hated her hair in plaits, but it was thick and wavy, and the only way she could get her hat on. As they walked into the kitchen, Rebecca's Mum gave them both a drink, and a packet of crisps.

"Thanks Mrs Woods." Phoebe said. While juggling the crisps and drink in her hands, as she walked upstairs.

In Rebecca's room, Phoebe opened her bag of crisps, and sat on the bed telling Rebecca where she had just come from.

"Wow, l wish l could be like your Mum, that's what l would love to do." replied Rebecca.

"Well, if you think that's exciting." Phoebe added.

"My Dad is going to be working on a new film soon, and it's all about a magical kingdom."

Rebecca asked what the film was going to be called, while trying to brush some sort of normality back into her hair.

"I think it is going to be called ''The Goblin King.'

"It won't be in the cinema until later next year." Phoebe answered. "Dad has to ride the horses they want for the Stunts." She added.

Asking whether she would ever like to ride in films.

Phoebe said, that she already knew what she wanted to do. To ride in the 'Olympics', was all she ever dreamt about. As they munched on their crisps, Rebecca asked if she wanted to play a game on the Xbox. As they looked through the array of games, there were lots to choose from.

"let's play a riding game." Phoebe said, taking another sip of orange squash.

So the two friends each picked a Famous Rider, and began facing all the challenges they had to endure, to get them through to the next levels. Phoebe and Rebecca soon showed off their competitive sides, and were both trying to become the winner. They eventually got fed up with trying to beat the Professional Rider, and decided to go on the Karaoke machine instead.

"Let's make out to be a new girl band on X Factor." Rebecca laughed.

After tying their hair up, while putting lipstick, and glitter eye shadow on. The two friends were singing and dancing. When suddenly, Rebecca's mum walked in, asking if they would like to go downstairs for something to eat. The girls were so embarrassed, that they made a quick exit out the door!!

"You would think you girls were starving." Mrs Webb laughed, as she watched them run downstairs.

As the girls sat eating sandwiches and cake, they giggled to each other. The thought of being caught dancing with a face full of makeup, and their hair sprayed with red glitter, was not funny.

As Soon as they had finished, they rushed upstairs to wash their faces. Sitting in the bedroom, Rebecca asked Phoebe if she was going to the 'County Show' next week, as it would be good if they could meet up.

Phoebe told her that she was, as she had entered Barney in the Cross Country. As time went by, they could hear a car tooting its horn. Going to the window to have a quick look, phoebe turned and said. That it was her mum, who had come to collect her.

"That went fast." Rebecca said.

"It must be six already" Phoebe replied.

Quickly making her way downstairs, Phoebe said her goodbyes.

"Oh, bye dear." Mrs Webb replied. As Phoebe rushed by.

"Tell your Mum l asked after her." She added.

"Will do." replied Phoebe running towards Mum, who was waiting in the car.

It wasn't long before they were soon back home. Teddy, came galloping up to the gate of the paddock as usual, as he recognized the car instantly, and knew they were back. Phoebe ran over, and began to stroke him. The rain had long stopped, and one of the staff must have let him out to be with Lolly.

"I will go and get your brush, you would like that wouldn't you boy." Phoebe told him.

She knew that he loved to be brushed, he would stand for hours if he could. Teddy loved affection, and she gave it to him. Once he was all groomed, Phoebe took him to his stable and went to get Lolly, who was waiting patiently by the gates to be taken in.

Lolly was such a sweet little thing, being only tiny, she would follow Ted everywhere. She reminded Phoebe of a big bear, because she had a thick cuddly coat in winter.

"Come on Lolly, let's get you in as well." said Phoebe, placing Lolly in the stable right next to him. Making sure they were alright,

She then walked over towards the barn where her father was. As Phoebe called out, she saw that he was standing with Apollo.

"Hi ya Phoebe." said Dad, as he brushed him. "Have you had a good day?" He added.

Phoebe nodded, and walked towards him.

"Yes l've had a great time." She replied, "How's Apollo?" She asked, turning towards Dad.

"His fine, in fact l am just getting them ready for an early start in the morning." He answered. "I have to be on set in Pembrokeshire tomorrow."

Phoebe turned to him and asked, if he was going to be away for a long time. Giving his daughter a reassuring look, he told her that it was only for a few weeks, and then he would be back. Turning towards him, Phoebe gave him a hug, and told him she was going back to the house, as she was freezing cold. Dad turned and said, that he will be in shortly himself, as soon as he had finished with packing.

Walking back, looking at barney and another pony further out in the paddocks. Phoebe spotted the ducks going home to their hut, and laughed to herself at the way they walked in a line, all following Daisy, who was definitely the boss !!

As she neared them, one of the ducks who was called Donald, run up to her like a little dog. As he walked right by her side, as if on a lead. Donald followed her wherever she went, everyone was amazed at the way he had attached himself to Phoebe. Dad had found them down by the lake when they were very young. Their mother had been taken by a fox, and scince then, they have only known Phoebe. But it was Donald in particular, who had formed this amazing bond, with whom he thought, was his Mother.

"Donald !!" she called out.

"We have to get you in, so you're safe from Mr Fox." She informed him. As she took him back to the others, and locked them in. Suddenly, Mum could be heard calling in the distance, so she made her way back to the house.

Standing by the kitchen door, she told Phoebe that she had made something special for tea, being as Dad would be leaving early in the morning. So Phoebe went to wash and change.

That night was really busy for her parents, what with her father having to leave early, and Phoebe going back to School.

Phoebe was looking forward to getting back. Some of her friends had gone on holiday abroad, and she couldn't wait to hear all their news. As soon as dinner was finished, she went upstairs to bed.

The next morning, as Phoebe went downstairs to the kitchen, Mum told her, that she had not long missed her father. But he will be ringing later when he gets to Pembrokeshire. Phoebe asked, who was at the front door earlier, as she could hear talking.

Mum replied, that it was Mr Grieves from the farm nearby. He had gone out to his chickens this morning, and noticed that he had been visited by a fox. All his best hens had been taken. So he had come round to warn them, to make sure that they started locking their chickens in at night.

Phoebe didn't like foxes attacking the animals, and certainly didn't want to see the fox get hurt because of it either. But sadly she had witnessed herself the damage they could do, having lost many of her chickens. But she quickly learned, that this was the way of the Country. Livestock, were too important for farmers to lose, so had to be protected. Sadly, even from the Fox.

Soon Alex and Holly entered the kitchen. They were waiting for her mother, to tell them what was on the rota's for the day. Mum, who had been getting her paperwork on the day's schedules, started to get breakfast ready with the help of Holly.

Mum always cooked for everyone that worked there, this was much easier. She could discuss the business of the day with them, as they sat around the table. Mornings were always busy and quite manic to Phoebe, but Mum liked to think of it as organized chaos.

With bacon and eggs sizzling in the pan, in came some more Staff ready for the day's work. Phoebe sat eating her breakfast, and telling everyone how she was looking forward to getting back to School. And informed them that there was a fox on the loose, So could they keep an eye on Donald, in case he wandered from the other ducks. She couldn't bare the thought of losing him like that.

Everyone loved Donald, and said that they would watch out for him. Besides, they knew what Phoebe was like with her animals, and they loved her for it.

Once at school, the Class were told to write an essay, on what they had done in the School holidays. Of course Phoebe wrote about the Horse Show, and how she had won rosettes with Teddy, Barney and Lolly. Others wrote about the holidays they had been on.

Soon it was lunchtime, and that gave Phoebe a chance to catch up with her other friends, as she wanted to hear all about where they had been.

Rachel Watts, had gone to Disneyland, Paris. Lorna Green, had visited her grandparents in Spain. While Jayden Holmes, and his brother Matthew, had gone on a Cruise Ship around the Mediterranean. Phoebe found everything so fascinating.

She had not been on holiday for awhile. Her parents had been so busy, that it had been impossible to go anywhere, apart from the few times they had gone to Hunstanton. Which was a Seaside Town, near to where they lived.

Lunch came to an end, and they were soon back in class, reading their stories out to the Teacher. Within no time at all, it was home time. As Phoebe came out of School, Mum was waiting for her by the gates.

"Hi Mum!!" Phoebe called out, running towards her.

"Did you have a good day?" Mum asked, taking Phoebe's School bag.

"Yes it was great fun." She answered.

"We had to write down what we did in the holidays." Soon, some of her friends had gathered round, to discuss what time their lesson was with Alex.

"You will need to be there for at least four thirty." Mum informed them. Phoebe told her friends that she will see them later, and said her goodbyes.

When they reached home, Mum told her to change, if she was going to have a lesson with Alex. As he was a stickler for time keeping.

After a quick change, and a slice of pizza, Phoebe went for her lesson...

Alex was waiting when she got there. He wanted them to continue with their jumping. But first they warmed up with *Around The world*...

(This meaning, taking your feet out of the stirrups, as you do a full turn around the horse, whilst remaining in the saddle.)

Once they had finished their balancing techniques, they then had to prepare for going over the jumps. As even though they had been riding for sometime now, it was easy to pick up bad habits.

"Lean into the saddle, and loosen the reins slightly when you go over!!" Alex called out to them, as one by one they jumped. Phoebe was quite pleased with herself that Barney didn't clip the rail.

"Well done." Said Alex. "You are learning to relax a lot more now." He added.

When her lesson ended, Phoebe took Barney for a canter around the paddocks. It was always good for him to go for a gallop, he enjoyed himself.

While riding back towards the stables. Phoebe saw Teddy watching, so dismounted Barney and walked over to him.

"Don't worry Ted, l will get you saddled up, and take you for a short ride." She said. Not wanting him to feel left out, she went to get his tack.

From the next field, Phoebe could see Rebecca having her lesson, while Megan and Casey watched on.

"Hey Phoebe where are you going?" shouted Lewis. Who was making his way towards her, on his pony called Branston.

Phoebe replied, that she was riding Teddy to the lakes, to give him some exercise.
He asked if he could join her, so off they both went.

Lewis began telling her, that he had entered Branston in the 'Cross Country' on Sunday.

Phoebe told him, that she had also with Barney, but was worried as it was her first time. Lewis told her it was natural to feel a bit scared.

"It can be quite daunting, when you see the course for the first time." He added.

Phoebe felt much better, with the knowledge that everyone experienced the same feelings. As they rode back near the stables, the others had already finished their lesson.

Calling out to them, she asked if they would like to come back to the house, before going home. They all turned and said that they would, and rode towards the yard.

After leading them to the inner paddock, where the ponies were to stay that night. The girls followed her back home.

"Hi Mum, could you make us some of your hot chocolate with marshmallows in?" Phoebe asked, as she entered the kitchen.

"We could really do with something hot to drink."

"Of course I can, you lot must be freezing, come into the warm." Mum told them.

Inside the kitchen it was lovely and warm, even though it was very large, was still quite cosy.

Being decorated in a typical farmhouse style. With oak units around the walls, and a huge wooden table and chairs in the middle.

Just opposite, was a small fireplace which housed the Aga, and sitting either side, were two comfy chairs that were great to snuggle up on.

As Phoebe and her friends were drinking their hot chocolate and eating some cake, the phone rang. It was Dad, ringing to let them know that he was okay, and had arrived safely. Once Mum had finished talking, she passed the phone to Phoebe.

"Hi Dad, how is everything there?" She asked.

"It's great, very wet and freezing." He replied, in a quivering voice.

Adding, that both Axel and Apollo were lovely and warm, which was more than he was.

"You look after everything there for me, until I get back." Dad told her.

"I will, and you take care." She said. Giving the phone back to Mum, she made her way back into the kitchen.

Telling her friends, that it was Dad, who was finally in Pembrokeshire filming 'The Goblin King.' And that hopefully they can start shooting tomorrow, if the weather gets better. The friends asked how long he would be there for, and who was starring in it.

Phoebe told them, that it would be for a few weeks at least, while filming took place. And that there was a few famous people, but she couldn't remember who her father had said.

"Will he be getting their Autographs for you?" Rebecca enquired. Phoebe told them, that he probably would, and that she already had a collection of pictures that had been signed by various people.

" l will show you if you like." Phoebe replied, and started searching through the kitchen drawer for her Album.

As her friends looked through the pictures, they saw her father with some of the most famous people in Films and Television.

As Mum came back into the kitchen, she told Phoebe that tea would be ready soon. And that it was time for the girls to go home, as it was getting late.

That evening after everyone had gone, Phoebe with Mum, went to check that everything was alright with the horses. Going into where Teddy and Lolly was, she could see them munching on hay.

Phoebe went up to Teddy who planted a big wet kiss on her face, and off he went, back to eating. That was typical of him.

Lolly being only tiny, stretched her head as far as she could towards Phoebe, who gave her a pat on the head.

She made sure she never missed a thing, which always made Phoebe laugh.

CHAPTER THREE

Walking off towards where Mum was seeing to the other horses. Phoebe walked past the paddocks, she could see Barney in the distance with the other horses.

He looked like he was enjoying himself, running around, as if he was playing some sort of chasing game. Mum came along with Alex, and some of the others who worked there.

They had finished for the day, and was saying their goodbyes. Phoebe went back inside with Mum, it was certainly much warmer than the bitter cold outside.

Yes, winter had arrived she thought, as she cuddled up to Mum by the fire. With its flickering lights of reds and oranges, the room was cosy, and made Phoebe feel all snug.

It was lovely just to sit there, after all the chores had been done. And was even better when it was cold outside. Phoebe thought how lucky Teddy and Lolly was, to have a thick winter coat of their own.

They certainly needed one in this weather. Winter, was always hard work. Contending with the rain, mud and even snow sometimes.

When water would freeze, and buckets needed filling by hand, it wasn't easy. The animals all had to come first before anything else. But Phoebe loved her life, and wouldn't want it any other way.

As she finished off her hot chocolate, she eventually made her way to bed.

The week went by quite quickly, especially now that the clocks had gone back an hour. It was like that at this time of year, when it would be getting dark by five.

Soon the day of the *County Show* had arrived. This being one of the most important Shows of the year.

With the Cross Country that lots of people had entered for, along with many other Competitions. One being, the Dog Agility, with dogs of all sizes competing, which was always fun to watch.

There were lots of other things, including Archery, a Steam Rally, and even Jousting. For those that loved to shop, there were the Craft and Gift stalls, selling everything from Equestrian wear to Jewellery. It was always a brilliant day out for families and their pets.

Phoebe was busy getting the horses ready, when Louise came along with Casey.

"Hey Phoebe, how are you feeling today?" asked Louise.

"I'm fine, a little nervous about doing the Cross Country, but l will be okay once l get going." She replied.

"It's great fun when you're riding around the course." informed Casey mumbling, as she was trying as hard as she could, to put popcorn in her mouth without dropping any.

Giving Casey a look of worry. Phoebe knew she would just have to go for it, and learn from her mistakes.

After walking the course, to find out where all the jumps would be. The girls discussed, the best way to get round in the quickest time. All too soon, it was time for them to get ready.

As other riders were told to go, the girls waited their turns. Rebecca was called first, after her it was Louise, and then Phoebe. Who was feeling very nervous by now, and just kept saying to herself... *I can do this... I can do this....*

As they came up to the start, she concentrated hard on the course in front of her, and as soon as the whistle sounded, Phoebe and Barney went off like the wind!!

Barney was in full gallop, when they came to the first jump. Which was made up of logs. But over he went with ease, as if nothing was going to faze him. The wind picked up by now, and brushed against Phoebe's face, which made her shudder. But she managed to keep composed.

Having a nice long canter until the next hurdle, gave Phoebe an opportunity to pace herself. But as she got nearer, the rain came down, and suddenly everything was quite different..

The course became wet and slightly muddy, up ahead, she could see the next jump, and this was the one that looked difficult. As she got nearer she kept thinking...

Should l take the easy way or just go over.

"Come on Phoebe!! She thought to herself.

"Make your mind up!! In a split second, she decided to take the easy route. Phoebe was getting soaked by now, and the ground was muddy and slippery. She gave Barney a quick reassuring pat on the side of his head.

Poor Barney she thought, he was just as soaked as she was. The lake by now was fast approaching, as she kept a tight grip on the reins. Phoebe started to enter the water...

There was a small log jump that lead up to the embankment, and as they went over Barney lost his footing!!

With her heart pounding, she kicked her heels in and managed to get Barney back up. It was so slippery where all the other ponies had been, that mud was over both of them.

"Good boy Barney, you can do this." She kept saying, whilst holding on tightly.

They were nearly at the finishing line, and she was feeling exhausted by now. Barney had really excelled himself, and she was just glad that they had managed to get round, with no problems.

As they went over the last couple of jumps, and galloped through the finishing line. Phoebe gave a huge sigh of relief!!

Mum was cheering away, and run up to Phoebe as soon as she was clear. Looking at the time, Mum knew that she stood a good chance of coming in fifth place, if no one could beat her.

Taking Barney to get unsaddled, and to give him a good drink. Phoebe sat on the steps of the horsebox, when after a while, along came Rebecca riding Blaze, looking very excited.

"Phoebe Adams, l think you may have taken third place!!" She shouted, as she jumped down from Blaze.

"No way, how come?" Phoebe asked.
Then Rebecca began to tell her, what had happened after Phoebe had gone through the finish line...

"Well Lewis on Branston had a fall, as they approached the sixth jump in. Louise didn't make the time, and Casey made it on second quickest."

"Who came in first ?" Asked a curious Phoebe.
Rebecca, who was looking rather pleased with herself, shrieked with delight. "MEEEEE !!"

Phoebe nearly fell off the step, she was so happy for her friend. Rebecca had been through such a rotten year with Blaze being so poorly. That it was great to see her finally achieve her goal, to win at *Cross Country.*

Gradually they were surrounded by the rest of their friends, who were all jumping and cheering with joy.

Mum came along wondering what all the commotion was about. When she heard, she was so happy for Rebecca, especially knowing all the problems with Blaze.
She never thought that they would be competing in Cross Country, let alone win.

While they all stood waiting to be called, to collect their rosettes, the friends all held hands. Phoebe took Barneys over to the horsebox where he was, and rubbed the side of his flank.

"Look, another rosette for you." Phoebe told him, as she stuck it inside the trailer next to him.

"Are you ready to make a move home?" Mum asked. Phoebe told Mum she was, and that Barney was already loaded.

When they arrived back, everyone at the School had heard that Phoebe and Barney had got third place. They had all come along to say *Well Done*. Phoebe said her thanks, and ran inside the house to wait for her father to call.

It was around six thirty that evening, when Dad phoned. He was amazed that she had came third, being as it was her first time, and told her how proud he was.

Phoebe began asking him how the film was going. Dad told her, that the Director wanted the horses to be able to do more stunts. But filming was on schedule, and so far everything was going well, and was keeping his fingers crossed that they would be home soon.

"How are the horses?" Phoebe asked.

Dad replied, they were good, and had been working hard on set. They were even being treated like Celebrities, which Axel and Apollo seem to be enjoying quite a lot. Phoebe laughed, saying, that when they come home, they will be expecting star treatment.

As Dad told her all about the stunts they had been working on, it all sounded very exciting. And then he continued to tell her, that when the film is released, they have been invited to the Premiere by the Director himself. Who had been so impressed by the horses and the stunts.

Phoebe squealed with delight, and began to tell him, she would have to buy a special dress.

As she came off the phone, she went back into the kitchen, dancing as she told Mum about the Film Premiere. Phoebe wasted no time, and began practicing her walk for the Red Carpet.

"Wait till l tell my friends at School." She said, while gathering her homework.

That night Phoebe found it hard to sleep. And as the next day arrived, she was up before anyone else.

Soon Mum came down from upstairs.

" you're up early." said a startled Mum to phoebe, as she walked over to the Aga, to start breakfast.

"I couldn't sleep that well, l have been thinking all night about what Dad said." She answered all excitedly.

Mum knew exactly how she felt, remembering the first time she had been to a Premiere. It all seemed so long ago, when Phoebe was just a baby.

Her father had been starring in a film about *'The Roman Empire.'* And was a stunt double for one of the main stars.

They soon became great friends, and when the film was released, was invited to attend the Premiere as his guests.

What an exciting night it had been too. With all the Celebrities, Television Crews and Reporters. Watching, as you walked along into the Theatre, believing you to be someone famous.

Mum smiled to herself, as it brought back so many memories, and looked over to Phoebe who was sitting by the table reading a magazine.

"Well Ms Adams, what would you like for breakfast today?" Mum said jokingly. Phoebe looked at her and replied.

"I think, l will have the full English today." Talking in a very posh voice. So with that, Mum prepared breakfast. Alex and Holly, and a few of the stable girls entered the kitchen, they had come to make an early start. Mum and Holly, made tea and coffee for everyone.

By the time it was eight thirty, Phoebe was ready for school. Walking along with Mum, she saw the School Bus turning into the School gates.

Phoebe turned to her and said, that she could run the rest of the way, as they were near the gates anyway. Mum watched until Phoebe went into School, and then walked back home.

In School, Phoebe wasted no time telling her friends about the Film Premiere. And that, her father should be home soon, as there was only a few weeks filming left to go.

When her Teacher, Ms Hills appeared. In a long grey cardigan, and pleated skirt, wearing her favourite pair of brogues. She told the girls to hurry up.

"Come along girls, no dwindling in the lobby." She said in her broad Norfolk accent, as she peered around the door.

The girls followed her into the classroom.

Sitting at their desks, Ms Hills continued...

"Today we will begin the morning with Science Studies." As she began to prepare the equipment, that they would be needing.

After the experiments the class had done, which involved making crystals from water. They then had to write a short essay on how the process was achieved.

By the time dinnertime came, Phoebe was happy. Science just like Math's wasn't one of her favorite subjects.

In the small hall, Phoebe lined up with the others to get their dinner. Rebecca asked what was for dinner.

"We have roast chicken, potatoes, vegetables with gravy today girls." said Gwen the School Cook, as she handed them their trays.

"What's for afters?" Casey asked, as she grabbed for the cutlery, looking over to see what was in the trays.

"Apple pie with custard." replied Gwen, giving Casey a large helping.

"Mmm.. my favourite." She said licking her lips.

As they sat around the table chatting away, whilst trying to eat, dinner time had soon finished. And they were back in class ready for their next lesson.

The afternoon went by quickly, and it was soon home time, and as the girls got ready to leave, they all decided they would meet later at *The Play Barn* at Guyhirn. It was a great place to go. There was a big ball park, with climbing frames, as well as slides and loads more. Everyone went there from School. Phoebe herself, had gone there many times for a friend's birthday party. The girls all agreed to meet at five that evening.

When Phoebe returned home with Mum, she ran upstairs and changed her clothes, and went to see Teddy, who was at the far end of the paddock with Lolly. Phoebe shouted for them to come to her. Galloping over at such speed, they nearly came through the rails..

"Be careful you two." She said, as she patted them on their heads. Then, jumping over, Phoebe started to brush Teddy down. Lolly kept pulling at her trousers, as if she was saying, *don't forget me.*

" Lolly, l will brush you in a minute" Phoebe said. As she stroked the mane out from Lolly's eyes.

Teddy was standing there like a huge bear. He had his winter coat now, and was all lovely and cuddly.

40

Phoebe loved putting her fingers through his thick coat, as it felt so soft. Once finished, she turned her attention to Lolly, and with her brush, started to get the dried mud out of her coat. Lolly made Phoebe laugh, the way she just stood there. It was like, Lolly had been Super glued to the spot, as nothing was going to move her away from that brush.

Once they were done, Phoebe walked them both over to the stable block. Giving them their hay, she shut the door and went to find Mum, who was taking a class of Adults for a hack around the outer paddocks. As she waited by the American barn, it seemed so quiet and empty.

Normally, the horses her father used for Stunts were there. Phoebe realized just how much she missed him. Dad was always laughing and joking, and was always telling her stories of the films he had worked on.

Walking along, looking at the empty stalls where Axel and Apollo would be, her thoughts were broken as she heard Mum in the distance.

Phoebe went outside to where Mum had dismounted from her horse, she was talking to the other riders, about the lesson they just had.

Waiting for her to finish, Phoebe stood waiting nearby.

"Come on Phoebe." Mum said, as she took her horse to the stables. "let's go and see if Dads phoned yet." She added. Phoebe followed behind her.

When they got inside the kitchen, Mum just put the kettle on, when the phone rang. Phoebe ran to answer it.

"Hi, is that you Lauren?" Asked a familiar voice joking.

"No it's me Phoebe !!" She laughed, knowing it was Dad.

"How's my favourite girl ?" He asked.

Phoebe informed him that they were well, and that she had been helping Mum, as promised.

41

"That's real good honey." said Dad, who then proceeded to tell her, that he had been riding for most of the day, and was very tired. Phoebe told him that she will go and get Mum. Who came to the phone, as Phoebe ran upstairs and quickly changed into a pair of jeans and a t-shirt.

It wasn't long, before Mum came upstairs to where Phoebe was. Telling her that Dad had sent his love, and will try and ring tomorrow. After Mum had a quick shower and change, they were soon on their way to guyhirn.

Listening to the Radio, as they went, the music was suddenly interrupted by a News Flash....

"A group of people have been arrested earlier today. As Police and RSPCA officers were called to a property late last night, after an investigation into reports of Animal cruelty. A spokesman for the RSPCA said "It was one of the worst cases he had seen." informed the Reporter.

"That's awful." said Phoebe looking at mum. "Why are some people so cruel?" She asked.

"I don't know that answer." Mum told her. "As l will never understand why myself."

By the time they reached *'The Play Barn'* the thoughts of what might have happened to those poor animals, were forgotten for a while. As Phoebe ran to her friends, right up high, sitting at the top of the climbing frame was Louise, who climbed down to meet her.

"Where have you been ?" Louise asked.
Phoebe explained, that they had to wait for a phone call from Dad.

"Well let's catch up with the other's now your here." Louise added, and off the two of them went. Mum was sitting chatting to the other parents, at a table while having a coffee, as Phoebe played.

By the time it reached seven, Mum was ready to get back home. Telling Phoebe that they had to leave, as the girls came back to the table, to get some more squash.

 Phoebe, who had been trying to beat one of her friends at Bowling, said her goodbyes, and left for home.

Reaching the Market Town of *Wisbech*, Mum asked Phoebe, if she would like 'McDonald's for her tea, as it would save her cooking. Of course, she turned and said yes please. And quickly made an order for a D*ouble Cheeseburger, Fries and a Chocolate Milkshake'*.

By the time they got to the village where they lived, it was very dark indeed. As they entered through the gates of the Riding School, Mum told Phoebe to take everything indoors, while she went to check that all was well with the horses.

Sitting in the warm kitchen, Phoebe sat eating her dinner, when the phone began to ring. As she answered, Phoebe recognized the voice instantly.

"Hi Penny." She said.

Asking if Mum was around, Penny said she needed to speak to her urgently. Phoebe explained, that she was outside checking everything was ok, and she shouldn't be long.

"Okay then, l will ring back in a few minutes." Penny replied. And with that, Phoebe went back to finish off her hamburgers.

 Soon Mum came into the kitchen. Saying, that all was well, and that Alex had left a note about something's, she needed to know for tomorrow. Phoebe told her, that Penny had just called, and that she was going to ring back in a few minutes. So while they waited, mum finished off her hamburger.

And it wasn't long before Penny soon rang back.

"Hi Penny everything ok?" Mum asked.

Knowing something was definitely wrong, by the tone of her voice. Penny went on to say, that she had received a call earlier from the Police. About some animals they had wanted her to help with.

"They have been so badly treated, and l wondered if you could come and look at some horses, that they had found there?" Penny said anxiously, waiting for an answer.

"Of course l will come." She told her.

"I heard something over the Radio tonight, is this related to it?" asked a worried Mum.

Penny began to tell her that it was, but she couldn't go into much detail at the moment, and gave her the address of where to meet her in the morning.

"No problems." Mum replied. "I will see you first thing tomorrow." As she entered the kitchen, Mum explained to Phoebe that she would be going to help Penny with some animals. They hadn't been looked after very well, and were in need of some special care.

Phoebe hated things like that, she loved all their animals at home, and couldn't bear to think of anything happening to them. Mum assured her, that only a small amount of people would be so cruel, and there were lots of people that cared for their animals.

That night, Phoebe curled up beside Mum on the sofa while watching tv, when Mum suggested they watch 'Mama Mia,' that always cheered them up. And she was right, as soon as the words came up on the screen, they sang as loud as they could.

The next day was horrible, it was raining and so windy, that the leaves were falling from the trees. It was the beginning of October, and winter had arrived with a vengeance. As Phoebe left for School, her mother went to meet with Penny.

CHAPTER FOUR

By the time she arrived at the Farm, the local Police were already there. Everything seemed so unreal at first to Mum, as she went to look for Penny.

A foul smell filled the air, and all around was rubbish and dirt. As she made her way through all the rubble, she noticed the horseboxes and trailers waiting to load the rescued animals.

In the distance, Mum spotted Penny, by what looked like some sort of makeshift stable, and walked over to where she was standing. As they walked in, there in the corner, were two foals that had been left in a terrible way.

Penny told her, that she had found temporary homes for the majority of the animals. And that she had taken in some goats herself. What she was desperate for, was a place where the foals could go. She asked, if it was possible whether Mum could take them to Silver Birch, once the Vet had given the all clear.

"If anyone can help these two, you can." Penny said, as she added "I could load them on the trailer and bring them to you later." Penny waited for Mum's answer, with fingers crossed.

She knew, it would be impossible for her to take anymore horses. The Rescue Centre was full to capacity. It had been a terrible time for horses and ponies lately.

"Of course l can, the quicker we can get them away from here the better they will be." replied Mum.

Penny said her thanks, she was so grateful that they would now be in the best possible hands. Mum left straight away for home.

Pulling her Staff together, Mum stood and told them how these foals had been found. They reacted the same way she had done, with sheer disbelief.

By the time Phoebe came home from School, Penny's horsebox was already in the yard. And as everyone stood waiting, the back doors opened, and the first sight of the foals hit them.

Thin, matted and dirty, showing all the signs of being badly undernourished, they struggled to walk. Their hooves were so badly overgrown, that it was heartbreaking to see.

Mum informed them, that she had already spoke to Tom, who was coming over first thing in the morning. There was no doubt in anybody's mind, that they had lived in this terrible state for quite awhile.

Terrified and nervous, which wasn't surprising for what they had been through. Mum encouraged them into the stables. Looking at the straw, and bedding beneath their hooves, they gradually laid down.

"You're lovely boys." Phoebe said softly, as she looked through the bars of the stall.

The foals were Piebald Cobs, with very distinctive markings on them. Mum asked Penny why the foals mother was not with them. And that's when she informed them of her fate.

The mare had been found to late to be rescued, she had been in a terrible way, and trying to feed the young colts, did not help her situation.

Phoebe shook her head. The thought of someone inflicting so much pain and misery, on a defenceless animal, was to terrible to think about. It made her feel so angry.

"Right." said Penny "The vet will be here again, first thing in the Morning." She informed them.

Trying to change the subject quickly. This had not been a good day for any of them, it had certainly been one of great sadness. Mum went back to Phoebe, who was still sitting with the young foals.

As she placed her arms around her daughter. She suggested that they should go in, as it was getting late. Phoebe looked up and asked, if the foals would be alright.

"I hope so, they're in a much better place now." She answered. As she took her by the hand, and walked her back to the house.

That night was very sad for Phoebe, she couldn't understand how anyone could be so cruel. And as she sat by her dressing table, she prayed that the young horses would pull through.

In the Morning it was extremely busy, Mum had been awake for ages. And had already checked on the new arrivals, who were doing well.

Phoebe was in the kitchen eating breakfast, and talking to Holly, who had to make sure that Phoebe got to School on time. When Mum entered the kitchen, telling them she was surprised to see that the foals had eaten all the feed that had been placed in with them.

"That tells me they are eating well, with no problems." She said, to reassure her worrying daughter. Phoebe was happy, and went to School feeling much better.

When she reached School, Phoebe told her friends all about the new arrivals. Her friends asked all sorts of questions.

"They are only staying with us until they have a new home to go too." She told them.

After School that day, Phoebe rushed home with Holly to see how the foals were doing.

When she saw Mum coming across the yard towards her.

"Hi Mum, how are the little ones ?" She asked.

Mum told her, she could go and see them, but had to change out off her uniform first.

As soon as she could, Phoebe rushed over to the barn. On entering, the foals were standing, which was a real surprise to her. All their hooves had been trimmed by Tom, and Mum had even managed to wash and brush some of their coat. It was wonderful to see, but there was still a lot of work to be done.

As she watched the foals, Phoebe could feel the tears that had fallen onto her cheeks, so she tried to brush them away before anyone could see. Mum placed her arms around her and said, that it was looking good, and not to feel sad.

But Phoebe's tears, were tears of joy not sadness. She knew that from now on, they would be in good hands with her mother. As she went to leave, she noticed one of the foals that was standing by the door. So she placed her hand by him, to see whether he would turn away.

But to her surprise he didn't, and started to smell at her hand, as if to make sure that it wasn't going to hurt him.

"You're friendly." She smiled, and began to stroke his mane, he seemed to like this, and started to rub his head along her arm.

"You have a friend there?" Mum whispered.

The other foal was more wary of everything and anything, especially that moved. And hid behind his brother for safety. As she pulled her arm away from the door, Phoebe went over to Mum, and asked what will happen to them when they get better. She assured her, that they will only find good homes for them. As Phoebe left, she walked over to the yard, Teddy and Lolly had already been taken in.

On entering the stable, she could see them eating from the haynets. Calling out to them, they came near the door to see what she had brought. Giving them both a polo mint, she turned and told them, how lucky they were to be loved so much. She knew, she could never let anything hurt them.

Just then Mum walked in, and asked her If she was alright.

"I was just thinking how funny Teddy and Lolly are, when they know foods around." She laughed.

Watching them both, trying to get an extra polo mint.

"You would think they hadn't eaten all day." replied Mum. Phoebe gave them both one last mint, and then they went back to the house.

When Dad rang, there was so much to tell him. How they were now looking after two new horses, and all the drama that had unfolded.

"It was all on the TV and Radio." Phoebe informed him.

"All the other animals, have gone too places that will look after them." She added.

Dad told her, that it was a good job that they had been there to take the horses in, and that he was extremely proud of them both. He loved animals, especially horses. He was always bewildered, how anyone could treat such a beautiful animal so badly. Soon he said his goodbyes, and told her that he will try and call later.

It was around teatime when Penny arrived to see the new foals. Mum told Phoebe too stay inside, as it was too cold for her outside. She didn't mind, she sat near the Aga with her feet curled up, reading a magazine about Celebrities. Phoebe was fascinated how their world, was so different to hers.

When they came back into the kitchen. Mum asked them if they would like something to eat. As she was going to dish up Dinner.

"That will be lovely, I haven't had time for anything today." Penny informed her.

The smell of the 'Shepherd's Pie' coming from the oven, was too good to turn down.

Phoebe came back down after washing her hands, as Mum and Penny served dinner, talking about all the things that had happened in the last few days.

"I am excited about the Film Premiere." Phoebe said, as she helped lay the table.

"Perhaps Apollo and Axel will get to walk down the Red Carpet too." giggled Penny.

Everyone laughed, at the thought of these two huge horses, being led in front of all the Celebrities. It was then, that Mum asked Penny to stay over for the night. The roads were getting very dangerous with the fog, and it would make sense. Penny said, she knew her Staff would be on duty most of the night, what with the new additions, so everything would be in good hands.

"I will give them a ring and let them know my plans, that I won't be back until morning." She said.

That night, they sat talking and laughing, it was just the tonic they all needed. Phoebe loved having Penny over. It was always great to hear her stories, on how she started the 'Horse Rescue' by accident...

Apparently, starting just by taking a pony in for someone, who couldn't afford to keep him. Then gradually being inundated by requests for help, from all sorts of people and Animal Charities.

"Never give up on your dreams." she told Phoebe.

"That's what keeps you motivated in life. I love and enjoy what I do so much, and that's so important in anything you wish to achieve."

As Phoebe lay in bed that night, she wondered if she would ever make an *'Olympic Champion.'* That was her dream, she wanted her parents to be as proud of her, as she was of them. They had achieved so much, in their lives.

Phoebe woke in the morning to the sound of people talking in the hallway, it was Penny leaving.

"Good Morning sleepy head." She called out as Phoebe came downstairs, still wearing her pyjamas. Saying her goodbyes, Phoebe proceeded into the kitchen.

Alex and Holly were standing by the table eating toast, and were discussing their classes that they had that day.

After breakfast, Phoebe got ready for School. When she arrived, everyone wanted to know, about the two foals.

"How are they doing?" Casey enquired.

Phoebe explained that they were doing really well, and that the Vet was going to call sometime today.

"Then Mum could let them out in the paddocks." She told them. "I think they would love to be outside."

Casey and Louise, both asked whether she will be at the riding lesson tonight.

"As we could go for a canter down to the lakes after." they said. Thinking this would be a great way to take her mind of everything.

"That's a great idea!!" Phoebe answered.

That evening the girls met up at the Riding School, and went to their class with Alex.

There wasn't much Alex didn't know about horses, and he certainly knew how to ride them when under pressure. He had been an officer with The Royal Horse Artillery, and so Ceremonial Duties where always expected.

On finishing his service, he became a Riding Instructor, specializing in many of the Equestrian sports.

"Sit up straight, and pace yourself." He said, while walking in the centre of the School.

"Count your strides before you attempt to jump!!" He shouted to them. "I am still having to remind you!!"

Alex wanted the best from his students.

He got that from them, they always gave a hundred percent. Alex was well known for being a great Instructor, and they were lucky to have him. People would come to the School from the next villages to be taught, just by him.

Soon he was telling the girls to let go off their reins, and with arms outstretched to the sides. Do a *'Rise and Trot'* around the Arena. Just to show, they were more than capable of being on a horse.

When they had finished their lesson, they decided to take the ponies down to the lakes for a canter. They all lined up on the pathway, as Phoebe shouted.

"Ready steady go !!" And with that, they all galloped towards the lakes..

Going through the outer *Pony Trail*, they went past Teddy. Who, on looking up and seeing Phoebe, started to gallop at full speed, towards where she was going.!!

Poor Lolly, was trying as hard as she could to catch up with him. The two Shetlands on reaching the end of the paddock, could go no further...

"Look at Teddy go!!" screamed Louise, who was following just behind Phoebe, on her pony called Hetty.

Lolly's little legs, going at such speed to catch up with him, was a very funny sight indeed. Not knowing where he was going, she decided to follow, in case there was any food to be had. The girls fell about laughing, while trying to ride. Casey overtook Phoebe, who was desperately trying to keep on Barney.

As Casey got to the lakes first, she punched her arms in the air, and screamed. "I've won!!"

By the time Phoebe and Louise came along, they asked her if she had seen Teddy and Lolly.

"I saw a pony galloping, but l didn't think it was Teddy, because he went like a mini rocket!!" Laughed Casey.

As the girls came back towards the paddocks, they could see Teddy and Lolly in the distance. Phoebe dismounted Barney, and called out to them. Teddy looked up, and started to come towards her, he looked stunning when he galloped. He always had such a lovely pace for such a small pony.

Coming near to where Phoebe was standing, she put her hand through the rails and said to him..

"Hey Ted, if only you had galloped like that in the Pony Race last week, we might have won!!"

Teddy made a noise, as if he was saying something back to her, as Phoebe laughed.

Getting back on Barney, she gave him a smile.

"See you later Ted." And off she went with the others, back to the stables.

As they were putting the ponies away, Mum called out to them, asking if they would like to see how the new arrivals were doing.

"Oh yes please." They all said together, and followed her to the stable block. Just before they went in, Mum explained to them to be quiet. As she didn't want to cause any unnecessary distress.

Inside the two foals were eating from their haynets, they looked so different to when they first arrived, and they had even put on some weight. Phoebe and her friends quietly made their way to where the two foals stood. They didn't shy away like before.

The foal that Phoebe had stroked, the first time she had seen them, came straight towards her, as if he remembered that very first meeting.

"Hi little guy." She whispered, as she held out her hand towards him. For the first time, since they had been at the School, the foal nuzzled into Phoebe with his head.

Phoebe began to stroke him, when the other foal came to see her as well. Mum and the others looked on in amazement at the foals with her daughter. She seemed to have a special gift with animals, and the foals sensed it.

Mum watched Phoebe, and began to wonder, if her daughter was the answer to help her gain their trust.

As the next few days went by, the foals grew confident. And it wasn't long before they were going outside. Mum decided, that when they have their first outing, she would place them in the outer paddocks, on their own.

With Phoebe's help she led them both outside. At first they were afraid, and didn't want to leave the security of the gate. But noticing the other horses in the fields behind, they began running towards them. Moving so gracefully as they galloped around, they definately had a certain quality about them.

As Mum and phoebe were so busy watching the foals, they didn't notice a familiar horsebox, pulling into the School. And it was only when they made their way back home, they realized it was Dad, and ran to meet him.

"How's my girls!!" Dad called out.

Running towards him, Phoebe stretched out her arms, as her father spun her around.

Dad turned and said, that he wanted to surprise them both. Walking towards Mum, he noticed the foals that were running around the paddock.

"Are these the guys you were talking about, they look great." Dad said, watching them chasing each other around.

Mum informed him, of how well they had done, and of the special bond the foals had developed with their daughter. He was not surprised, Phoebe always had that something special about her. Anyone could see, animals seem to attach themselves to her.

"Come on let's go and get something to eat, l bet you're hungry?" Mum asked them.

But Dad had to unload the horses first, being as it had been such a long journey. As they neared the horsebox Josh was bringing out Shadow and Spirit, they were two American Quarter Horses. The breed being known for their speed and toughness. Were normally used in many of the Stunts involving Stagecoaches. But this time, Dad had taken them for other Stunts.

As Dad went onto the horsebox, out came Apollo and Axel. They looked amazing, as soon as they noticed Mum and phoebe, they made a loud neighing noise.

"We have missed you guys too." Phoebe told them, as she tried to put her arms around them both.

"Come on, let's get them settled in." Dad said to her. Phoebe walked along with him, and as they went passed the paddocks, all the other horses knew they were back. As they seemed to be talking to each other.

"I'm so glad your home." She told him.

"So am l, it's great to be back." He replied.

Once they were settled in, they all made their way back to the house, as Mum made a start on something to eat.

As they sat in the kitchen eating sandwiches with cups of tea and coffee.

Phoebe began to tell her father and Josh of all the things that had happened, while they were away. And her father in turn explained, all about the film they had been working on...

"It's all about a magical place, which has been destroyed by an evil king. Axel is a gift to the Elf Prince, and was a horse that talks.. It's all done by special effects, which looks brilliant!!

"Apollo was a Unicorn, who has to gather, all the animals of the forest together, to fight the Evil Goblin king."

Phoebe listened intently to her father, as he told her more about the film...

"We had to train them both to do all different kinds of Stunts. Myself and Josh, had to ride Shadow and Spirit in the fight scenes."

He explained that as soon as they get a release date, they would find out more about the Premiere. Phoebe couldn't hide her excitement, everything sounded so fascinating.

After they had eaten, Dad and Josh went to look on the horses, while Mum with Phoebe, went to see the foals, to bring them back into the warmth of the stables.

"They are gonna be mighty fine horses." Josh said.
As he stood looking at the new arrivals.

"Yep, they sure have that certain something about them." replied Dad.

"Exactly what l thought." Mum added.

That night, as they sat around the big open fire while toasting marshmallows, they talked about the two foals. Phoebe loved having Dad back home.

They chatted and laughed until quite late, with all the funny things that him and Josh were telling them. Everything sounded so interesting.

Phoebe told him, that Penny had stayed over, and that they had a fun evening watching old movies.

"That's good, I'm glad you had someone here." Dad answered, as he sorted through his paperwork.

It was always the same when he had been away, the invoices and receipts, all had to be checked out. By the time Dad had finished, her and Mum were already upstairs getting ready for bed.

Phoebe fell asleep quickly that night, the week had been so busy, that it had left her feeling exhausted.

The next morning Phoebe lay in bed. It was a Saturday, so there was no School. As she lay there, she was listening to all the noises coming from the yard. Thinking to herself that it must be late, as all she could hear was the sound of children's voices coming from the Riding School.

It was the younger children on Saturday mornings, and they would normally be using the Shetland Ponies.

As Phoebe came down to the kitchen, no one was around. So after doing herself some cornflakes, sat looking out the window. Seeing the Indoor Arena opened. she remembered her mother had a Class, and that she was teaching the younger ones today.

Phoebe decided to get her wellies on and go outside, to see if she could find any of her friends, or to see what her Dad was up to. Walking past the yard it was really busy, weekends normally were. With owners coming along to see their horses. Phoebe went over to the Indoor School, and on looking inside smiled, as she saw Teddy with a young girl riding on him.

She watched as he took the small child around the School. He was always so patient, and understanding for a little pony.

The moment reminded her, of when she first started to ride. He was her first pony, and she loved him to bits. Phoebe smiled as Teddy came past her, looking so proud of himself.

Making her way to the barn, she saw Axel and Apollo standing there. They both made neighing noises as Phoebe walked towards them, she knew they were only after one thing... a carrot !!

Just then her Dad and josh came along, they had just put the other horses into the paddocks and were coming back for them.

"Hi Phoebe what ya up to?" Josh asked, while placing their head collars on.

"Just giving them both a carrot." She answered, as she passed the last carrot to a very inquisitive Axel, who had been waiting so patiently for his.

"Are you going to take them outside?" She asked.

"Yep, once they're rugged up." Josh told her.

Dad came back, and asked if she would like to walk Apollo out. Walking along with Apollo, she looked so small against him, as he towered over her.

Taking his head collar off, he galloped around the paddock chasing Axel. Soon they were rolling around in the grass, it certainly was funny to watch.

Apollo and Axel, did what Phoebe called a dance routine, it was great fun to see. Dad went over to his horsebox and started to clean his things out, as Phoebe went over to help.

"I'm gonna go ridin' later, do you wanna come with me?" He asked her.

"We can go up on the Horse Trail by the river, if you like." Phoebe nodded and said she would love to go.

As soon as the horsebox was all tidy, they went to catch up with Mum.

"We are going up on the Trails." Phoebe said delighted, as she run up towards her.

CHAPTER FIVE

Mum told them, that she had just one more lesson, and she could go with them.

"It will be good to give Jade some exercise." replied Mum.

Jade was a beautiful Palomino, that Dad had bought her as an Anniversary present. Being specially shipped over from America as a surprise.

Mum was so thrilled, as she had always dreamt of owning one, from when she was a little girl.

later that day, after Mum had finished her Class, they went and got their horses.

Coming out of the Riding School, they made their way up to the Trail. Phoebe could see a Heron standing with his feet in the water, looking for a fish to catch for his supper.

It was beautiful up on the Trails, you could see for miles. With only the sound of the birds chirping away, it looked so peaceful. Through the trees you could see 'Silver Birch' nestled safely between them.

Even though 'Silver Birch' was a lovely old building, and had been renovated, inside was still in keeping with its charm and character. And was decorated in a style to accommodate Dads Antiques, that he had collected from around the World. But mostly what he had shipped over from America.

As Phoebe looked, she could see the Stables, paddocks and the lakes, that Dad had made for the geese and ducks. In the distance, the gardens which were private, and was a place where her parents could relax, away from the Riding School. It also had a vegetable plot, Summer house, and Phoebe's trampoline over in the corner.

From the trail you could see the Silver Birch trees, they looked beautiful as the bright sun shone through the leaves. Yes, it truly was a special place, and you could see why her parents had fallen in love with it.

As they came up on the bridge, they could see the fishermen, that were all along the bank trying just as hard to catch something, like the heron.

Dad said Hello to them, but as they neared a small woodland, they heard a loud bang which spooked the horses.

"What was that !!" said Phoebe her voice trembling, as she tried to keep control of Barney.

"I don't know, but I am gonna find out." He told them. And rode off towards the woods.

In the distance, he could see a group of boys who were playing with fireworks. As he called out to them, the boys ran away.

Dad told Phoebe, how dangerous fireworks were in the wrong hands. Sometimes they even throw them at animals, and at people, thinking it's funny.

But there were always fireworks around, before Guy Fawkes night. Even though, it was coming up to *Halloween.*

When they all got back to the Riding School, Dad told her to stay on the fields around the School. Especially with those boys hanging around.

As they unsaddled the horses, Phoebe turned Barney out into the paddocks, and walked up to the yard where some horses were being groomed by their owners.

"Phoebe where have you been?" Turning to see who was asking, she saw Louise. On telling her that she had just been out on a hack with her parents, she then began to inform her, about the boys playing with fireworks.

"Dad told the boys off and they ran away." said Phoebe.

"The other night we could hear fireworks, they were so loud." Louise informed her.

"Teddy hates them, we have to shut him in." Phoebe replied. Louise nodded and said, they did the same with Blaze.

Louise asked Phoebe, if she was still going to the *Halloween Disco* at the village hall. Phoebe answered that she was, as most of the girls and boys at School would be there. Louise told her, that she already had her costume, and that she would be going as the Bride of Frankenstein. Phoebe laughed.

Halloween was one of the big events in the village. Everyone would decorate their homes, with pumpkins and ghostly figures. The Riding School was no exception.

As the girls went up to the house where Mum was sitting in the kitchen by the Aga.

Mum asked, if they would like some hot chocolate.

"Yes please." They both answered.
They told Mum, about the *Halloween Disco.*

"You'll enjoy that, it's a good night." She said bringing the two hot chocolates over.

"You better start making your costume, if you're going then." She told Phoebe.

After Louise went home. Mum and Phoebe got to work on making the Vampire Costume..

The dress was made, from an old purple one that Mum didn't wear anymore. She had even managed to cut out some bat shapes, from a black velvet skirt, that had been hanging up in her wardrobe for quite sometime.

And using her trusty sewing machine, that was always handy to have on occasions like this. Mum sewed the bats all over the dress, and added some black lace around the hem.

61

With the last piece of material, she made a long purple cloak. Soon the outfit was finished, and after putting her fangs in her mouth, Phoebe tried the outfit on. It looked splendid, and Mum gave her the thumbs up.

The night of the witching hour soon came, all the houses were decorated, and the whole village looked fantastic. Mum had made some Halloween bags for the Staff to take home, and had laid on a fine spread. Consisting of sausage rolls, and sandwiches, and a chocolate fountain. That had lots of goodies to dip in.

Dad and Josh entered the kitchen, with some other members of Staff. While Mum poured out some of her *special punch*, as they helped themselves to the array of food.

Once the horses were all taken care of, Alex and Holly came in, they had brought their outfits with them. The house was buzzing with everyone having a good time. Phoebe entered with her Vampire outfit on, looking really scary. Mum had done an excellent job.

"Don't forget we have to go by eight-thirty." Mum told them. "We can take some food up to the hall with us." She added.

During the night, they were visited by lots of children, who had dressed as Witches, Wizards and even Ghosts. Phoebe and Mum stood outside, to let the children take the sweets from a cauldron, that Dad had made with an old bin.

And, as it got nearer the time of the Disco, everyone had changed into their Costumes. Phoebe thought, how strange they were all going to look, walking through the village. The thought made her laugh. As they reached the hall, Phoebe caught up with her friends from School, who had all won some prizes.

"We have been apple bobbing." they told Phoebe.

There were lots of things for them to do. Outside had many attractions, where they could win prizes. Phoebe saw Dad and Josh throwing Horse Shoes, so went with her friends, to Dunk the Witch.

When they got there, they picked up wet sponges from a bucket of cold water, and began to throw them at the poor old Witch. Who was sitting high up on a swing, with her legs dangling above a pool of water. She looked so funny as they threw the sponges, while she desperately held on. The girls couldn't stop giggling.

Louise asked them, to go with her to the Hook a Duck stall. So they went to see, if they could win a prize.

After awhile with her fishing rod in hand, Phoebe managed to grab a duck.

"Look l won !!" She shrieked all excited.

The Man on the stall, gave her a small doll dressed as a Witch. The girls fell about laughing, as they had spent most of their money, trying to win a supersize picture of One Direction. Making their way back inside the hall, the disco had started. Mum took some photos, as they danced to the music. Suddenly they played some Abba songs, and everyone got up to dance, even Phoebe and Mum took to the floor. The night ended, with the Best Fancy Dress Costume, which was won by a boy. Who was dressed as *Frankenstein.*

It was soon getting late, and Phoebe was beginning to feel tired. All her friends had mostly gone, so Mum and Dad decided to make the move home.

When they got back, Mum had prepared rooms for those staying over. As Phoebe went straight upstairs without even being told too. It had been a long day, and she was beginning to fall asleep. As Mum came upstairs, she went into Phoebe's room.

With the posters and pictures, of horses and popstars all over the wall, she saw Phoebe lying on the bed.

"Come on, let's get you in properly, sleepy head." And she gently helped Phoebe change for bed.

Covering her with a duvet, Mum saw her pictures of Teddy, Lolly and Barney beside her bed in a *'Best Friends'* frame. She remembered how excited Phoebe was, as a toddler to have Teddy.

They were inseparable, and if her daughter had her way, she would have slept in that stable all night beside him.

Mum laughed to herself, as she turned the light out.

The next day, Mum had already cleared up, with the help of Holly, and some of the others who had stayed over. And was already on her way to the stables, when Phoebe came downstairs.

"Morning." Mum said, as she was putting her coat on.
Phoebe asked if she could help with the foals.

"Of course you can" Mum told her, and with that Phoebe went to get ready.

Going towards the stables, they started with Teddy and Lolly first. Phoebe had always been told, that if she had animals, she must be prepared to care for them.

It was her responsibility to feed them, and to clean them, when needed.
But when she had School, one of the Staff would normally do this in the mornings.

As she grabbed Teddy, she walked him outside. Tying him to the post, she began to brush him. Teddy looked lovely and after placing his rug on his back, led him out to the paddocks.

"There you go Ted, you will see Lolly in a minute."
But as Phoebe let him go, he went into the paddock and rolled around on the muddy grass.

"It's a good job you have that rug on, after l have just brushed you Teddy!!" She shouted, with her hands on her hips. Teddy came back to the gate, and waited for Lolly like he always did.

With her bright pink rug on, out walked Lolly. And as she ran into the paddock, Teddy chased after her. Phoebe and Mum laughed at Lolly giving him the run around, until he finally caught up with her. You could watch them for hours, but Phoebe had other chores to do.

Following Mum with the wheelbarrow, they started cleaning out the Geese, Rosie and Jim. It was a good job they were busy by the lakes, no one could get near them but Mum. Otherwise, they would make a loud noise, while flapping their wings in protest.

Once they were cleaned, they went over to the ducks. Donald came running up to Phoebe as usual, getting under her feet.

"Donald be careful, you will trip me up." Phoebe said, as she tried hard not to tread on him. Daisy could be heard making quaking noises, as if she was telling him, 'come back'.

At the other side of the paddocks, the foals were waiting to be taken out. So Phoebe and Mum went over, to put their rugs on. They had settled in really well, and was use to being around the other horses. Soon it would be time to rehome them. As they let the foals into the paddock, Phoebe and Mum, was joined by Dad and Josh. Who had been watching them gallop around.

"You know l been thinking about those two." Dad said rubbing his chin. "We could give these guys a good home, we have plenty of room, and besides, they sure have taken to Phoebe."

Listening to what Dad had said, she was overjoyed.

Phoebe began telling her parents, how she would do her best to look after them. Dad was right, there was plenty of room here at Silver Birch. It would make sense, especially after all their hard work. No one wanted the foals to go.

Mum looked at Dad and told him, that if he was sure it would be a good idea, then she was all for it. And would inform Penny straight away.

"They will grow into great lookin' horses." Dad said. looking at the foals.

"They sure will." Josh replied.

"And it will take a special kinda person to bring the best in them out." Dad said, looking at Phoebe.

"I can do it, if you and Mum help me!!" She replied all excited, her parents nodding their approval.

The next few weeks would be a tense time for Phoebe. She would have to wait, to see if they could officially be the new owners. The court case was still going on, and all she could do was keep her fingers crossed. Seeing the foals from when they had first arrived, and how much they had improved. It would be very hard to see them go.

That night when Phoebe went to get Teddy and Lolly, she sat with them for awhile. Letting them know, they could soon have two new friends, if all goes well. Teddy nuzzled up to Phoebe, and she in turn cuddled up to him. It was as though he was telling her, that everything would be alright. For a pony, he always sensed when she needed a friend. Because when Phoebe needed someone, he was always there for her.

When she came back into the kitchen, her parents were going through some paperwork, while Josh was sitting on a chair nearby reading a letter. As he looked up, he told her that it was a letter from home. His mother had written to say, that his father and brother had been on a Cattle Drive.

"Wow that sounds exciting!!" Phoebe said, as she sat on the arm of the chair.

"There's nothin' like bringin' in Cattle, it's exhilarating." Josh added. "You sleep under the stars, and you spend most of the day in the saddle." He told her.

Sounding like, he was missing home.

"Yep, it sure is hard work." He said. "But at the end of the day, your job is to protect that herd, and bring them in safely." He added, folding the letter up, and placing it in his shirt pocket.

Phoebe asked him, if her father had ever been on a Cattle Drive. And he began to tell her, that her father was a true Cowboy.

"He could lasso a Steer from his horse, and have it ready for branding in seconds, nothin fazed your Pa." said Josh as he sat back down in the chair.

Phoebe told him, of the photo's she had seen of her Dad when he was younger. He was wearing his Cowboy hat and boots, standing around loads of horses. Her Nan had even sent some photos, of when he worked the Rodeo Shows, riding on the Steers.

"Your Daddy could ride a horse like no one else, he could make that horse do anythin' " said Josh.

"You watch your Daddy and your Ma, and learn from them." said Josh, as he went to pour himself another cup of coffee.

"They will teach you all you need to know about horses." He added. Just then Dad came over to Phoebe, and asked if she was okay.

"I'm fine, Josh was just telling me about your Cowboy days, when you use to be in the Rodeo's."

Dad smiled at her and said.

"You know Phoebe, when we get some free time, I will love to take you to the Ranch back in Montana."

Phoebe loved the idea of dressing up as a Cowgirl, and riding across the Plains. To even get the chance to visit her Grandparents, and all her Relatives that lived there, would be brilliant. That night when she lay in bed, she dreamt of being on a Cattle Drive with her father.

Phoebe woke up feeling great the next day. And couldn't wait to get to School. She told all her friends that her Dad wanted to keep the foals. And that she might even go to America, to visit her Grandparents in the New Year.

For Phoebe, it seemed such a long time since they had been away together as a family, she was so excited.

After School, Phoebe told them that she will catch up with them later, at their riding lesson.

That evening, the girls went over to the stables as usual, to get their ponies ready for their lesson. As they entered the School, Alex was waiting for them. He was just putting on his jacket, ready to put them through their paces.

"Dressage, is all about the control of the horse, using subtle movements for command." He told them.
So one after the other, the girls had to show what they had learned so far. Phoebe wanted to learn everything, it was important if she was ever going to get a chance, of being in 'The Olympics.'

After the lesson, Phoebe asked her friends if they wanted to come to her home. The girls nodded and said they would. Mum was preparing dinner for later, when the girls walked in. Phoebe told Mum, that they were just going upstairs for awhile

"Okay, but tea will be done soon." Mum replied. As she placed a saucepan of potatoes on the Aga.

As they sat on the bed the girls started talking about School, and the boys in their Class.

"Brandon has lots of girlfriends." said Phoebe.

"Yes, but Harry is much better, he likes horses." laughed Megan, who was busy brushing Casey's hair. Phoebe turned and said, that when Harry came dressed as a Werewolf for the Halloween Disco, it was so funny.

"At least he dressed up as something scary, the others just came as Pirates." said Rebecca, while looking in a mirror trying out her latest lip gloss.

"Well Jayden and Matthew came as they were!!" Casey said.

The girls fell about laughing.

As they were chatting away, Phoebe's Mum could be heard calling them from downstairs. It was Rebecca's Mum who had come to take her home.

"Bye Becks see you at School." The girls shouted out to her.

As Rebecca left, Mum told Phoebe that she will take the other girls home. As it was getting dark now, and she wanted to make sure that they all would get home safely.

"Okay, we'll be down in a minute." She replied.
The girls went to get ready to leave, just as the phone began to ring. As Mum answered the phone it was Penny, with the news that they had all been waiting for. She had got permission, to rehome the young horses with them.

Mum was so relieved that it was all over, and couldn't wait to tell everyone. She was beaming with delight, when Phoebe came downstairs with the rest of the girls. And, on seeing her Mother's face, Phoebe asked If everything was alright.

"Yes everything is just great Phoebe." She said.

With tears in her eyes, she called out to Dad, who came running into the hall. As they all stood there wondering what was wrong. Mum told them, that they were now the proud owners of the foals !!

Phoebe and her friends screamed with delight, and jumped up and down with joy. It had been a long, and sometimes heartbreaking experience, for all of them to be involved in. And now, it had all been worthwhile, they now had two extra horses to take care off.

Mum thought that it would be a good idea, if they all went to see the firework display, when it is held on the village green.

As this would be a great way to celebrate their news.

The firework display was held on the village green, and everyone went. There was always a huge bonfire, and a fairground. On stage, local bands would play.

Phoebe couldn't wait for the weekend to come. She knew, that it would be the perfect way to share sometime together.

When Saturday arrived, Phoebe with her parents and Josh, walked up to the Village Green. You could see the entire Fairground, all lit up in different colours.

The smell of hotdogs wafting through the air, and the bonfire ablaze.

Dad held on to Phoebe's hand as they walked near to the Stage, where a country and western band was playing. Dad with Josh soon started singing along to the songs.

"That's sure good music." Josh turned, and said. As he stomped his feet to the sound, of a *Billy Ray Cyrus* song.

Phoebe watched, as her father enjoyed himself.
Mum asked, if they wanted some Hog Roast, of course they all said yes. So Phoebe went with her to get some.

CHAPTER SIX

While there, Phoebe bumped into her friends who had just arrived. They were all going over to the Fairground.

"Are you coming over to the Rides?" asked Megan. "It's okay, my sister has come along to look after us."

Phoebe turned to Mum who smiled, and said that it will be alright. But to remember, she had to meet them back at the stage, before the fireworks were lit.

Off the girls went, and as they reached the Fairground, they saw Rebecca and Louise, who had already been on the *Waltzer*. They told Phoebe and the others, not to go on if they had just eaten.

"It's all that spinning that makes you feel ill." Louise said, with her hand on her stomach, looking very pale as if she was going to be sick. Phoebe suggested, that perhaps they should go on the *Dodgems* first. As they went over to the ride, they could see sitting in the cars. Harry and Brandon, with Jayden and Ben.

"Look who's sitting in the cars." shrieked Megan.

"Let's show them how to drive." Phoebe said, with an attitude. And with that, the girls paired up, and each got into a car.....

Soon Phoebe was putting her foot down, and trying to catch Harry and Brandon. While Rebecca laughed hysterically. Suddenly, they were bumped in the back by Jayden and Ben. As their heads went forwards, Phoebe tried to get control of the wheel. Jayden and Ben laughed, as they went passed.

"You wait, we will get you!!" shouted Phoebe.
Shaking her fists in the air, as Rebecca continued to laugh.

As soon as Phoebe managed to get the car moving again, they saw Megan with Louise coming along.

"Quick.. let's get them!!" Rebecca screamed.

Phoebe started to gain speed, and soon they were right behind them. When suddenly.....BANG!!

They were hit in the side by Harry and Brandon. Phoebe, struggling to get control of the car, went straight into the back of Jayden and Ben!!

She couldn't believe her luck, and said calmly to them.

"Told you we will get you."

Soon the ride was over, and the girls were laughing as they got out of the cars. The boys quickly followed behind them.

"Look, let's go on the Waltzer, they won't go on that." Louise said, as they ran to get in a car.

With the bar down, the girls held on tight, as a Man came to take their money.

"Hold on tight, I want to hear you all scream !!" The man in the booth said. Soon the ride started picking up speed, as it went round and around. The friends laughed, as they were all being squeezed onto Phoebe. Who by now, was desperately trying to move them back.

Faster and faster the car spun around, as the girls were screaming for it to stop!!

As the ride began to slow down, they noticed the boys standing there laughing.

"Typical !!" Phoebe said, with her cheeks glowing red with embarrassment, and trying to compose herself.

"Just like them to think we look funny."

The girls then made their way to *The Octopus*. With eight long arms, each holding a spinning car. Megan and Phoebe jumped in. Louise and Rebecca shared the next one. As the ride started, a man who worked there, spun the car around as fast as he could.

Making the girls feel a bit queasy. Going high in the sky, they could see the entire Fairground, the Bonfire, and where the Stage was.

A cold evening breeze brushed against phoebe's face. Sitting high up, in a little car that was spinning, made her stomach take a jump.

"Oh no...My stomach feels like it's in my mouth!!" screamed Phoebe, as the ride came down again.

The two friends could see Rebecca and Louise, screaming in the other car.

"We must be mad!!" Phoebe screamed to Megan. Who by now, was clenching her fists around a small bar, that seemed to be the only thing, that was holding them in. As the ride started coming to a halt, the girls were only too glad, to have their feet firmly back on the ground!!

As they rejoined Phoebe's parents, who seemed to be enjoying themselves, dancing along to the Band playing on Stage. Mum asked them, if they had a good time at the Fairground.

The girls all said they had, and told her all about the Rides they had just been on.

Dad showed Phoebe a big teddy bear, that he had won on the Rifle Range, and gave it to her.

"Wow, thanks Dad." She said, taking the teddy from him. Dad told her, that being as she could never take the real Teddy upstairs, this was the next best thing. Phoebe laughed, she knew what he meant.

Soon a man came on stage, and told the crowds that he wanted to thank everyone who had turned up, and added.

"We are now going to have our firework display, so please enjoy."

And with that, there was an almighty bang!! As rockets went up in the sky, whistling as they went.

The fireworks were so loud. Phoebe had great difficulty trying to keep her fingers in her ears, while holding a great big bear. Smoke filled the evening air, as fireworks went in all directions. Suddenly a loud bang was heard, and as Phoebe looked up, there in the sky, was a shower of beautiful stars.

Soon the evening ended, in a wonderful display of colour. What a great night it had been, they all thought.

"I haven't laughed so much" Phoebe told them.
Mum turned and said, that she hadn't danced so much.
It had just been what they all needed. It had been such great fun....

When Phoebe woke the next morning, she looked outside the window. There was a thick layer of fog, that swept across the paddocks like a blanket, she couldn't see anything past the stables. Coming downstairs, Mum was cooking breakfast and dad was sitting reading the Sunday papers.

"Have you seen the fog outside, I can't see any of the horses." Phoebe said to them.

"They are fine" Mum told her, she had already been outside to make sure that they were alright.

"I will go and see them once l get dressed." said Phoebe.

"You will need to wrap up warm then, as it's freezing out there." Mum told her.

Phoebe soon finished her breakfast, and went to get ready. Putting on her thick woolly socks over her jodhpurs. She then put the knitted jumper on, that Dad had brought back from Pembrokeshire. It was lovely and fluffy, and had two Shetland Ponies on the front.

Quickly putting her coat and boots on, she walked outside. Everywhere smelt of smoke from the bonfires, and as she walked into the stables, there was Teddy.

"Hi Ted, here's a carrot for you." She said.

"And one for you too Lolly." She added, as she walked over to Barney, making sure he never got missed out.

As she sat there, she began to tell them of the great news.

"You have two new friends coming soon!!" Phoebe said. Letting them know, that they will now be keeping the foals. Phoebe didn't want Ted to think she didn't need him anymore.

He was the most precious thing that she owned. Teddy gave her a reassuring look, and Phoebe cuddled up to him. Just then, Phoebe heard mum as she came out into the yard. She asked Phoebe, if she could help bring the foals over. They were waiting patiently in their stalls.

Placing head collars on them both, they walked the foals over to where Teddy, Barney, and Lolly was. Mum told phoebe that she will let them settle, before she did anything else with them. Phoebe said she will stay with them for a while, to make sure they were okay. Mum knew she would, and left her with them.

Sitting there, Phoebe could see how wonderful they were beginning to look. She sat with them for quite sometime when Dad came in.

"Phoebe you still sitting here?" He asked, kneeling down beside her. Phoebe looked at Dad.

"I just wanted them to know they were going to be alright now." She answered, as she continued to stroke them.

"I'm sure they already know that honey." he said.

Placing his arms around her shoulders.

"Come on inside it's cold, they will still be here tomorrow." He added. Looking at the foals, Phoebe turned and said goodbye to them, and walked back home with Dad.

In the kitchen, Mum had made a lovely dinner. And as they sat eating, Dad turned to phoebe, and began to tell her the story of his first ever pony.

75

"He was the most stunning lookin' pony that I had ever seen. My Pa had brought him back from Dakota, from the Cheyenne Indians that live in settlements there."

Dad taking another sip of coffee continued....

"That pony was given the name 'Wild Spirit,' as no one could go near him, let alone ride him. He would've probably ended up being sent away, if my Pa hadn't brought him home. Everyday I would go and watch him, as he paced up and down along the Corral. Sometimes, he would gallop around at such speed, like if he was looking for a way out.

Then, one day when I was playing outside, near to where he was. That pony broke free, and tried to make a run for his life. Where he was going, to this day I will never know.

But suddenly for some reason, he stopped running, and came straight back towards me. Probably to stand his ground, too see what I would do...

At first I was pretty scared, but he just stared me straight in the eyes, like if he was checking me out. And then, he did the most remarkable thing. He walked right up to me, and placed his head straight upon my hand.

I was trembling, and as I went to pull away, my Pa, who had been watching nearby, told me not to move. You see, he had seen something special in me, and he believed that I could help that pony. And he ended up being right, because that pony had felt that same thing, that he hadn't with anyone else.

He had learnt to trust me, and for that, became a great horse and friend." Dad turned to Phoebe and added...

"That's what I see in you Phoebe, that same thing my Pa saw in me, those two foals are already trusting you. They see no reason to be afraid anymore."

That night, Phoebe kept thinking about what her father had told her, and she knew that she must believe in herself. That she could achieve her dreams.

The next few days were spent watching, and learning from both her parents. These were to become the most memorable, and rewarding times of her life...

It was soon the beginning of December, and there were no more local shows, until the following year. But this had given Phoebe and Mum, time to work with the foals. Who had grown quite a lot, in the last few weeks.

They were becoming very striking, and typical of a Vanner Cob. With heavy set bodies, and thick feathering on their legs, they would look great as Carriage Horses, just like her father had pointed out.

The days were getting colder and very dark quick. The Riding School was now closed until the New Year. So Mum concentrated on the livery side. It was the time of year when the weather was awful. It would either be raining constantly, or just so cold.

Alex and Holly, had gone to their homes for the Christmas holidays, and there were only a few people left at the yard. This gave Dad, time to work on Axel and Apollo, with new routines. Phoebe would stand at the outer paddocks, watching her father and Josh, doing their stunts with the horses. Showing her, what great horsemen they truly were.

Axel and Apollo always made everything look so easy, the way they moved gracefully, when practicing new routines. Shadow and Spirit, would also race around the paddocks.

Being ridden bareback at such speeds, that it would make Phoebe catch her breath in fear for her father. People that came to the livery, would stand and watch them in amazement.

Phoebe herself, would try hard to copy her father. She would stand in the paddock, trying to practice on Teddy. Whose only interest would be, trying to see what food he could catch. It did make Mum laugh, the sight of Phoebe trying to get him to do anything.

It was a lovely relax atmosphere at the yard, it gave Phoebe and her parents time to be together, as normally Dad was working away on films, and Mum would be busy with the School and Livery.

Although it was like having a big family, when everyone was there, for Phoebe, she would have loved to have had a brother or sister. Someone she could share things with. But Phoebe considered herself lucky, she had met people from all walks of life, because of the Riding School.

As the days went by, Mum decided it was time to get the house ready for Christmas. She wanted the decorations up. So Phoebe and Dad, went to get a Christmas tree for the house, one they could plant in the garden after.

They drove all the way to a town called *Swaffham,* to get their tree. While there, Dad decided to get a couple of ducks. Thinking, this would be a nice surprise for Donald and Daisy. And so, they ended up in the local Poultry Auction.

But, being as it was an Auction, Dad ended up with more than just ducks. They suddenly accumulated more chickens, and geese. Phoebe wondered what Mum was going to say, when they got back.

Coming out of the auction, they went to pick up their tree from the local forestry, and made their way home. Pulling into the drive, Penny's jeep was there.

On entering the kitchen Phoebe said *Hello, Penny* was saying how well the foals looked. Phoebe informed Mum, that Dad had taken the tree of the trailer, and was going to take it straight into the Sitting Room.

The room looked perfect. With the fireplace all draped with holly and ivy, entwined with pinecones, the decorations looked lovely. Mum had done a good job, she always made her own garlands, fresh from the trees in the garden.
Mum decided, that they will decorate the tree that night.

Mum asked Penny, If she would like to stay for some dinner and help.

"Oh yes thanks, l would love to" Penny told Mum.

"I'll just nip back home, and get a few things". She added.

Dad called Mum and phoebe outside, to see the Christmas lights, which he had placed around the yard. It all looked beautiful, even the trees outside near the front of the drive, had been decorated with different coloured lights.

Mum was so surprised at what Dad had done, that when he showed her the new ducks, geese and chickens. She didn't really say that much. Besides, he had done such a good job with decorating the School.

Phoebe nodded to her father, she knew he had got off lightly, and was very lucky.

That night, Phoebe and her parents were making popcorn strings to place on the tree. A tradition that Dad always did, from when he was a young boy back home in Montana. Christmas carols played out on the radio, and everyone sung along.

As they entered the sitting room, Dad had lit the fire, the room felt lovely and warm. Mum brought in some eggnog for them to drink. And once the tree was all decorated, Dad switched on the lights. The tree looked beautiful, with all the baubles and glass ornaments on the branches.

Sitting around the fire listening to carols, it made Phoebe feel good, she loved Christmas.

It was the time of year when they were all together, and that meant more to her than anything. After everyone had dinner, they all sat talking.

Mum, knowing that Penny was on her own now, scince her husband passed away. Asked her to spend Christmas with them again.

There was plenty of room, and she was now considered part of the family. As time went by, Phoebe made her way to bed, she had School the next day, and wanted to get up early.

The next morning when Phoebe got up, the place wasn't as manic as it normally was.

The few Staff that was there, had already been told what was to be done. And when Tom the Farrier came, Mum had given him a basket full of goodies, for all his help and support throughout the year.

At School, the nativity plays were being rehearsed. Phoebe was playing one of the *Three Kings*, along with Rebecca and Jayden. Harry, Louise and Matthew, were the Three wise men. While Megan and Henry, were to be Joseph and Mary. Poor Phoebe, she had to wear a false beard, a long gown, and a crown on her head.

"I have to wear this beard!!" she shrieked, feeling very dubious of the fact, she would be wearing this on the night.

"we are going to look stupid, dressed like this." Rebecca said, as she looked at the pair of them in the mirror.

As they walked into the hall for dress rehearsals, you could hear Ms Hills telling everyone their places.

"Don't forget to practice your lines at home." She told the class. Phoebe couldn't wait to get that beard off.

It was itchy, and the thought of having to wear it in front of the boys, made her feel even more silly.

"I am glad that's over with" She said, taking her gown off.

"At least them two, know we look funny." Rebecca said.

Pointing to Harry and Matthew, who were laughing over in the corner, finding the whole thing hilarious. When School ended, Phoebe and the girls arranged to go to *Kings Lynn*, for a shopping trip. They could get presents, for their friends and families there.

Lynn, as it was known locally, was an old Sea Port, which had still maintained many of its Historical Buildings. There was even an old Goal, which the School had visited once.

The boys had took it upon themselves, to be put into the Stocks, just to see what it was like to be a prisoner for the day. But Kings Lynn was the ideal place for Shopping, with the Market, and many of the High Street Shops.

Mum told Phoebe and the girls that she will take them, and that they could meet up at The Quay Side. Where the coffee and tea shop was, overlooking the river.

Later that day, when the girls went looking in the various shops for presents. They could hear The Salvation Army singing carols. As they went over, they could see a sleigh which was being pulled my two horses.

"Look, Father Christmas is coming!!" Louise shouted all excited. The girls went up, and placed some money in the buckets being carried by people dressed as Elf's.

And then went on their way.
looking at the array of market stalls, with various goodies, they soon finished their shopping.

And went to meet up, with Phoebe's Mum.

"Are you finished." said Mum. As the girls sat down exhausted from all their shopping.

"Yes, l have bought something for Ms Hills, and for Penny." said Phoebe, showing her a printed scarf with horses, and a box of Aromatherapy Bubble Bath.

"That's great." said Mum, as she got up to get the girls a drink each. After a hot chocolate, they started their way home. Gradually the girls were dropped off at their houses, until it was only Mum and Phoebe left in the car.

As they drove along the busy road. Mum turned to Phoebe and said.

"What a year it's been Phoebe, we have now got two new additions, the foals. And we have been invited to see the film, that Dads been working on."

"Yes that will be so exciting." Phoebe answered.
She also reminded Mum of the other new additions to the household, all the geese, chickens and ducks, they now have.

"Yes, l forgot about them, l have your Dad to thank for that!!" Mum replied. As she went on to say, how well Phoebe had done at the Shows. With Barney turning out to be just the right pony, to teach her, and Teddy and Lolly, also doing them proud. Phoebe turned and said, that the best thing of all, would be next year, when they could visit her relatives out in America.

"Yes, that will be great." Mum replied.

As they reached home, it started to snow. And as the car stopped, Phoebe jumped out, trying to catch the snowflakes with her hands. Dad and Josh came out of the barn, and went to meet them.

"Looks like we are having a white Christmas after all" said Dad, placing an arm around Phoebe.

That night Phoebe lay in bed, thinking of all the things that she had been up too, and all the new things that lay ahead. To ride Barney in a *County Championship*. And to train the new horses for carriage driving, with Dads help.

By morning the snow had settled, and looked like a picture on a Christmas Card. The whole village had been covered with a dusting of snow, and looked so beautiful.

Phoebe couldn't wait to get outside, she loved the snow. As she came out into the yard, she ran to where the horses were. Teddy and Lolly was chasing each other around, licking at the snow. The two new foals, were a bit wary of the ground being covered in a soft white stuff, and looked funny as they attempted to walk on it.

Over in the distance, she spotted Donald and Daisy with the new arrivals, all trying to walk in a straight line on the frozen lake. As Daisy seemed to be enjoying herself, giving them their orders

Just then, her thoughts were broken by Mum calling. Telling her to hurry up, as she would be late for School. It was the last week of term, and Phoebe dreaded the Play. But at least she had her friends with her.

As she looked around watching the horses, her father and Josh over at the barn, putting Axel and Apollo out into the paddocks. She realized just what a special place 'Silver Birch' was.

Phoebe, had been lucky to have met so many different people, that had come into her life. That it really didn't matter anymore, that she never had a brother or sister. She had all the family she needed, right here.

Walking over to Mum, they began the short walk to School. Phoebe could see right across the fields, they were laden with snow, and looked so beautiful and peaceful.

As they came to the village stores, Mrs Anderson who lived on her own nearby, was just coming out. Carrying a small basket of groceries and the Daily Newspaper.

Turning towards them, she said politely.

"Morning Mrs. Adams, Morning Phoebe."

Mum and Phoebe said *hello*, while trying to rescue her Jack Russell dog. Who had somehow managed to get himself all tied up, on a nearby shrub.

"Oh no, is such a naughty boy, he's always after something" said Mrs Anderson, as she struggled to keep hold off her dog. Mum turned and said, that if she needed anymore groceries, to just let her know, and she will take her.

"Oh thank you dear, l will do just that, before the weather gets bad." replied Mrs Anderson.

"It will save me taking Monty out." She added, as she looked down at the little dog, who by now was sniffing at the basket, to see what goodies were in there.

Mum and Phoebe watched as Mrs Anderson, tried to keep hold of the little Jack Russell, as she walked along the icy pavement.

Continuing their walk to School. Phoebe was thinking how caring Mum was, especially to the villagers. Some of them were on their own, and didn't have anyone. And in times like this, when the weather was bad, it was just natural for Mum to offer help.

Phoebe had nothing but admiration for her parents, everyday brought something different. That's how it was, there had never been a dull moment living at Silver Birch.

As she entered the School gates, Phoebe watched as her friends played outside. They were having a snowball fight.

Louise came running up to her, she was covered with snow. Saying they were having a battle with the boys, and needed her to come straight away. Phoebe laughed, she knew this may all end in tears for one of them.

Running to where her other friends were waiting. She quickly began to defend herself from the barrage of snow, that came from the boys side. As they continued throwing snowballs at each other.

It all became clear who was winning. The boys did have an advantage point, of being behind the hedging.

The girls were beginning to resemble Snowmen, and were certainly relieved, when the bell went for them to go in. As they entered the School, they dusted the snow from their coats.

Still arguing in the Cloakroom that the boys were definitely cheating. Ms Hills told them, that dress rehearsal for the School Play will be straight after registration. Which made Phoebe cringe. This was something she was not looking forward too.

As Ms Hills went through the names in the register. Phoebe looked outside the window. From her classroom you could see the Church, and the surrounding houses. They looked so beautiful all covered in white. Phoebe was in a world of her own, when suddenly she heard.....

"Phoebe Adams, are you with us today?" Ms Hills enquired. Sitting bolt upright in the chair, Phoebe replied she was, her face going bright red in colour.

"That's good." said Ms Hills, putting her glasses back on.

As she finished with the registrar, they were told to make their way into the hall. On Stage, all the preparations for the play were still going on.

Some of the Mums were still painting the Scenery. While others, had offered to finish sewing the Costumes they would wear.

Ms Hills told them to change, as this would be a full Dress Rehearsal. Phoebe wasn't pleased, that she would probably have to spend the majority of the morning wearing a beard.

Sitting there watching the younger Class, dressed as Angels and Stars as they sang *'Oh Little Town of Bethlehem'*.... Made the whole of Phoebe's Class sigh, they looked so cute.

Soon it was Matthew and Jayden's turn to stand on Stage, to tell the story of Christmas. As she listened, Phoebe soon realized, that they had put gobstoppers in their mouths. Because, every so often, they would get them stuck in their cheeks. making them look like giant hamsters.

Ms hills soon caught on to why the whole Class were giggling, and promptly made them remove the offending sweets.

The rest of the Class made their appearances, as the story went on. Until it all ended, with the whole School singing *'Away in a Manger'*.....

Phoebe and Rebecca were the first two back in Class, to remove themselves from those beards, which was such a relief. Especially after hearing every joke, from Harry and Matthew. Ms hills told them that playtime would be soon, and to make sure they change into their wellington boots, when going outside.

As the bell sounded, out into the playground they went. Gathering up as much snow as possible, the girls started making their snowballs. Ready to attack the boys.

But as they were about to move into position, they suddenly caught Harry and Matthew spying on them. With snowballs going everywhere, the girls bombarded them.

Falling about laughing, they were pretty pleased with themselves. And was rejoicing in a minor victory when the bell went....

Quickly lining up, as if they were the innocent party, the girls stood waiting for their Teacher. Harry and Matthew, looked as if they had met their match. Covered in snow, with their hair all wet, they stood in a line. The other boys all curious to know what had happened to them.

Phoebe and her friends laughed, it was about time they got justice for all the jokes they had endured.

Ms hills came outside, and looked at them both amusingly, not even asking what had happened, and ushered the Class inside.

Sitting by her desk watching, as the two boys were struggling to dry their hair, with blue paper towels. Phoebe giggled to herself. She didn't mean them any harm, and the boys had taken it all in fun. They had even asked for a rematch.

Looking around at Rebecca, Louise, Casey and Megan. She knew she was lucky to have such great friends. And even the boys were brilliant at times.

As Phoebe sat there, she began to think about all the things she had to look forward to in the coming year. It was all so exciting. And she wondered what else would be in store for Phoebe Adams. We will just have to wait and see, she smiled to herself....

THE END

11670779R00050

Printed in Great Britain
by Amazon.co.uk, Ltd.,
Marston Gate.